D0504965

Gun Dogs and the
Countryside

Gun Dogs and the Countryside

Hunter Adair

ROBERT HALE · LONDON

© *Hunter Adair 2009*
First published in Great Britain 2009

ISBN 978 0 7090 8556 0

Robert Hale Limited
Clerkenwell House
Clerkenwell Green
London EC1R 0HT

www.halebooks.com

The right of Hunter Adair to be identified as
the author of this work has been asserted by him
in accordance with the Copyright, Designs
and Patents Act 1988.

*A catalogue record for this book is available
from the British Library*

2 4 6 8 10 9 7 5 3 1

Typeset in 11/14½pt New Century Schoolbook
Printed in Great Britain by the MPG Books Group,
Bodmin and King's Lynn

About the Author

Hunter Adair has lived and worked in the country all his life. He was born in Ayrshire, Scotland, in 1933 and brought up on a farm. He was educated in Scotland and studied agriculture at the West of Scotland Agricultural College at Auchincruive near Ayr.

In 1959 Hunter joined the Milk Marketing Board for England and Wales, working at their cattle breeding centre in the North of England. In 1965 he was appointed Regional officer in the northern region, covering the north of England up to the Scottish borders, where he visited estates and farms. He was also editor for one of the company's farming magazines for a time. Hunter worked for the company for a total of thirty years.

At present Hunter runs the family farm at Hexham, Northumberland. He also sometimes writes articles for the *Newcastle Journal*, the *Hexham Courant*, and the *Northumberland Farming Journal* about farming, wildlife, game shooting, gun dogs and the countryside. He was a runner up as NFU Country Person of the Year 2002.

Hunter has written several popular books for both children and adults, on farming, wildlife, gun dogs and the countryside, largely illustrated with his own photographs, drawings and paintings.

Contents

Illustrations

Introduction

I have had dogs around me all my life, especially gun dogs, and have learnt a great deal about these animals. To get into a dog's mind you have to be with the dog a lot to pick up certain signals.

A good gun dog will soon pick up any weakness in his master or trainer and try and take advantage of this.

I have worked and trained gun dogs for over sixty years, mainly springer spaniels and Labradors. I also have a long history working with a variety of collie and terrier dogs on the farm. Some of the gun dogs I have trained I have pushed really hard to see what they were capable of. Another gun dog I would work very hard until it dropped exhausted. This gave me a lot of information about the dogs and is not cruel, as some gun dogs will hunt and run themselves until they drop if not stopped, just for their own pleasure.

Once I had this information about a gun dog it helped to manage it in all conditions and get the best out of the dog.

I spend a lot of time with gun dogs. Some gun dogs will talk to me with their body movements and actions which I soon pick up. There are stories throughout the book about gun dogs talking to me.

1

Training Your Gun Dog

We may be a nation of animal lovers in the UK, but this isn't always a good thing. Some people have no idea how to look after the animals they keep, and through an unwitting combination of ignorance and benevolence, cause their animals a degree of cruelty that is very difficult to understand. But it is all done in the name of love!

For instance, I recently read about a Labrador dog that weighed seven or eight stone because it had been overfed for some time. This dog would certainly undergo great stress simply from trying to get around and walk. Its food intake should be gradually reduced to get the dog's weight down, and its owners should start giving it some exercise. Those owners probably never thought they were doing the dog any harm – indeed they would have thought they were being kind to it. But lack of knowledge and understanding of the dog meant that they couldn't see the harm they were doing to it.

I have seen lots of gun dogs at work in my lifetime, and a great many of them were overweight, though not to the same extent as the Labrador I've just mentioned. Sometimes the dog's owners would say they knew their dog was a bit overweight, and what did I think? I would ask how often they fed their dogs, and some would say, 'Twice or three times a day. Is that too much?'

My first response is to say, 'Look at your dogs. They are telling you they are getting too much food. That's why the dogs are so heavy!'

Some owners might turn round and say, 'It is my wife's fault the dog is too heavy. She is always feeding it titbits.' Or the reply might be, 'It's the family that keeps feeding it. I keep telling them to stop, but they don't take any notice of what I say.'

When a gun dog is living in the house with a family it *is* very tempting to give the dog a little snack when it's your tea time. But when the dog lives out in a kennel, then the temptation is not there to give it that little snack. However, my gun dogs have always lived with the family, although there are strict rules laid down about the dogs' behaviour. They are not allowed to sit on chairs or any household furniture, and they also have their own bed and food and water bowls.

PUPPIES

My gun dogs are trained from puppy hood to understand what their place is in the household. This process takes time and patience, but the more time you spend on it, the quicker the puppy will get to know what's wanted of it and get to know what it can and can't do.

They should be fed twice a day, close to their sleeping quarters, and their eating dish removed afterwards.

Young puppies should be confined to a small space while they are being house trained, and this space can be extended as the puppy's training progresses.

At both morning and evening meals the food should be gulped down, the dish removed, and the puppy then should be offered a drink of water, a little bit of which should be left in the puppy's dish all the time, but not so much that they can splash it around and make a mess.

A puppy should be given sufficient food to satisfy its appetite. If it doesn't clean up its food in a few minutes then you have given too much food; you should cut down the amount until the puppy cleans up its food quickly.

Look in at the puppy a few times a day and take it out to a grass area if you have one, or into a yard or a sand pit if you have made one, and stay with the puppy for a few minutes until the puppy empties itself. The more time you spend taking a puppy out to empty itself, the quicker you will get it house-trained.

OLDER DOGS

Gun dogs soon get to know when they get fed and will look forward to their next meal. I find it is enough to feed my adult dogs once a day, whether they are at home or working out in the field. When I am out shooting and we finish up and get home about 6 o'clock at night, the first thing I do is feed my dog.

I give it enough food to satisfy its appetite. How much is that? It is quite easy to measure. After my dog has been working out in the field all day I measure into its dish a quantity of food that I reckon it should be able to gulp down in a few minutes. If I find the dog struggles to finish this, then the quantity was too much, and the amount can be adjusted. When the dog is not working in the field its food can be cut down, then I remove the food after the dog has been fed. The dog should then be offered a drink of water, and some water should be left in the bowl, especially if it's warm weather.

I know I have said it is not a good idea to give a dog a little snack or biscuit from time to time, especially when it is living in the house with the family, but it is very tempting. I am probably as guilty as anybody at giving my dog a little bit of something it likes from time to time: a biscuit or a tit-bit maybe. However, although I do this, I am very careful what bits I give my dog and when, because if you have a dog in the house and a mealtime comes round, the dog will come and stare at one or two of the family hoping to get a titbit. And if you or other members of the family have been giving the dog a little snack on a regular basis, it will soon catch on to this and get up from its bed and hang around where the food is being consumed.

This is a very bad habit, and if a gun dog continually gets scraps to eat at human meal-times, as well as its regular feed, it will soon put on weight, and this can lead to all sorts of health problems for the dog. (When gun dogs are kept in kennels away from the house there is much less chance of their getting titbits and biscuits from members of the family.)

EXERCISE AND OBEDIENCE

Gun dogs need lots of exercise when they are not out working in the field. I try and give mine an hour's walk in the morning and the same in the afternoon, and they are not allowed to hunt while they are out for exercise, unless I am having a training session with them.

A keen gun dog will always want to hunt no matter where you take it. If you are out in a park or a wood it will hunt in every little bush or shrub to see if there is any game in there. But don't let your dog go and hunt like this for its own pleasure. Call it up, because this is your leisure and play time with the dog, and you should give it a short training session or two as part of your fun and play time.

You may have to be quite firm with the dog if it keeps wanting to hunt in every bush it comes to. Remember the dog is bred to hunt, but it should not do so unless the trainer or owner instructs it to. If you take your dog into a field or park where there are no bushes or shrubs this will reduce the temptation to hunt. You are trying to mould the dog to do what you want it to do and be obedient all the time. This takes time, lots of time, but the dog will catch on to what it has to do if you are consistent with your training and simple instructions.

To help make your dog obedient when you are out working or exercising it, keep it close at hand all the time. This is most important. If you have to, keep the dog on a long leash, or have a measured bit of string or cord – and you can extend the string or cord as the dog begins to get the message to stop, come back, sit or heel as instructed.

Don't let your dog range any further out than about thirty metres from you, then call or whistle it. The dog should then turn and look to see what you want. Then you can signal what you want it to do. If you want it to come to heel, signal that to the dog and make sure it does it. If you want the dog to range or hunt out to the right, signal that to the dog as it turns to look at you, and do the same if you want the dog to hunt out to the left. Make the signals simple and clear.

You can use a dog whistle or hand signals or your voice. If you are training a gun dog, or even if the dog is just a family house pet, you will get much more pleasure from it if it does what it's told when it's told. In fact that's the secret of having a dog that you can take anywhere and it won't let you down – and you will have a lot of fun with a dog like that.

With most dogs that are family pets (whether they are of a gun dog breed or not) and are not used for working or showing, it is fine to use voice commands. You can also use hand signals and a dog whistle if you wish, just so long as you make the dog do as it's told.

But using voice commands with working gun dogs is a different matter. While you are training a dog you can use your voice to reinforce hand signals and whistle signals, but when you are working it in the field among game birds and ground game, then if you have to shout at it all the time you will scare all the game for miles around. Game birds and ground game will soon pick up your voice and either fly off at high speed or run away from the voice – and if the weather is calm and quiet they may well end up in the next county.

You can use your voice quietly when your dog is working close at hand, but when it is any distance away from you it is better to use whistle and hand signals as these will be less likely to scare any game that lies ahead of you.

I use a dog whistle, hand signals and my voice when I am training and working my gun dogs, but you have to get to know just what signals to use and where your dog is. Even when I have a dog out just for some exercise I often have a short training session using all three signals just to get the dog used to stopping, starting, sitting and coming to heel in response to all of them when it is still close at hand.

(It is pointless trying to train a gun dog if it is half a mile away from the trainer or in the next county.)

EARLY TRAINING

With a young puppy that is to become a working gun dog, or just a family pet, I start training when it is about ten weeks old.

I first take the puppy and tell it to 'sit'. When it has done so I take a few steps back and see what happens. If the puppy comes to me without being called I take it back to the starting point and make it sit again at the same spot. As I continue with this process (which does take some time) I also start using hand signals in addition to my voice, and I start with a dog whistle.

This simple early dog training can very much try your patience, as there are not many young puppies that will sit and stay when asked to. They will either keep coming to you, or they may go off in a different direction. So keep at it until the puppy gets to know what it has to do. You can gradually take a few more steps back from the sitting puppy until you are several metres away, and it doesn't move until called.

On no account must the puppy move until called, for these first training sessions will stay with the dog when it is out working among the temptations and distractions of game and ground game in the field. And at these early training sessions the trainer must be utterly consistent. A young, excitable dog, eager to get going, may find the training a bit boring, but as the training sessions continue and develop they will instil automatic habits in the young dog.

I have trained some young, nervous gun dogs in the past which weren't very easy to teach. When I asked such a dog to sit, and then tried to take a step or two back from it, the dog would often come and shuffle around my feet.

If a timid young dog comes around your feet when called at a training session, don't punish the dog. Take it back to the same spot and make it sit again, then take a few steps back, and if the dog again comes shuffling among your feet repeat the procedure. Be persistent with this training, as it will eventually come, and the dog will get the message about what you want. On the other hand, if you punish a young dog for not sitting when told to, it may bolt, and this will make the training more difficult. Some young nervous dogs I have trained in the past have turned out to be very good gun dogs, though not ideal gun dogs.

What you can try when you have a nervous puppy that won't sit when asked, is to hitch a bit of cord or string to a peg or post and tie the puppy to the cord; if the puppy moves to come to you, the cord will check it, and in time the young dog will get to know what's wanted. In such cases I normally use a dog hitch with a bit of string tied to it that just allows the puppy to come forward a little, and it should stay when told to.

The dog hitch I use is just a metal bar about seventeen inches long with a corkscrew twist at one end and a ring at the other. It is easy to carry around in the field, and when I want to use it I just screw the hitch into the ground and tie the dog to it. This sort of gadget is used by lots of gun dog enthusiasts in the field if their dog is inclined to run in after shot game birds and pick them up without being told to. (There are lots of gun dogs that run in because they are not properly trained, or haven't had enough training to try and prevent it, and even the best-trained dog will sometimes forget and run in after a shot game bird or decide to chase a rabbit which runs across in front of it as it sits beside its master.) Some game shooters who have a young gun dog and hope to give it a retrieve or two when they shoot a few pheasants get very annoyed with owners of dogs that dash in and pick up the bird they have shot.

Most of my trained gun dogs have at times taken a risk, thinking to themselves, 'Let's take a chance,' and have dashed off on the spur of the moment to check something out or to flush some sitting game birds in the hope that they might get away with having a chase. Sometimes when I have been walking on a rough shoot and a hare or rabbit has been flushed, my dog might dash after it for a few metres, then, realizing what it was doing, pulled up smartly and quickly returned to heel.

If a dog is any use as a working gun dog it should always be looking at taking risks and chances when it can, hoping it might get away with some of them when its master is not paying full attention. I like gun dogs that I have to keep watching all the time when I am with them in the field, dogs that take the first opportunity they see to take a risk and do their own thing. Indeed, some dogs you have to shut up in the vehicles or sheds or tie them up at lunchtime, or they will be looking around to see where they could go off hunting on their own.

The problem is, though, that gun dogs which run in after shot game birds or ground game without being told to can spoil a shoot. A shot pheasant may drop into thick cover on ground that is due to be part of the next drive, and if one or more dogs run in to pick it up, they can flush unshot game birds sitting there and so ruin the next drive. The same sort of thing can happen on a grouse moor when shooting over dogs. A dog or dogs running in to pick a shot grouse that dropped a long way out in front of the guns can flush other sitting grouse in all directions, and, since these will be well out of range of the guns, part of the shoot will be spoiled.

A dog that is quite steady is less likely to run in when it sees a shot bird fall to the ground. It is more likely to look at its master to see what he wants it to do (though there is no guarantee that the dog won't run in when it's least expected). I have trained steady gun dogs in the past, and it has been great fun working with them.

Whether you have a dog that is always pushing to get out there and hunt, a timid dog or a steady working gun dog, when it is out working among game it will step up a gear or two, and the real dog can be studied.

I once had a springer of my own, called Bob, who was liver-and-white. My father had bred him and I had taken him on to train when he was just a puppy. He was a very strong-willed dog, and while I was training him for work in the field we had many scrimmages to see who was going to be in charge. But when he wouldn't do what he was told I went back to what my father taught me to do: keep the dog close at hand, go back to the start of the training again, and be consistent. Thus it was established that I was the boss and then our brains became attuned to each other. I then started to give Bob more scope, knowing now that he would respond to my instructions. Then, when he was about fifteen months old I took him to a few pheasant shoots and joined in with the beaters, keeping him on a rope a few metres long, just to let him see what he would have to do. At the end of a drive I sometimes let him off the leash and got him to retrieve a dead pheasant or two, just to give him experience and build up his confidence.

Because of his very strong will, though, Bob was always looking for opportunities to do his own thing, and I had to watch him all the time in the field. My father and I knew we had a brilliant gun dog but it was a matter of controlling his wilfulness and developing his skills.

I used to give Bob more scope to range and work at our own shoots than I did at other game shoots, where I kept him under stricter control to try and stop him from embarrassing me by his strong actions. And when the shooting season was finished I continued taking him out twice a week throughout the summer for refresher training to keep this brilliant, strong dog keen on his work but also under control.

I always use what is known as a silent dog whistle when training my gun dogs. The whistle is not really silent, and I adjust the tone to the point where I can just hear it, and then I know that if I can hear it, so can the dog.

I use one chirp of the whistle to stop the dog and two chirps to call it to heel. If I want to attract the dog's attention when it is working some distance away from me, I give a few sharp chirps on the whistle and the dog will look round to see what I want. I can then direct it with a hand signal to hunt in whichever direction I want it to.

2

Reading Dog Signals

Some time ago I used to shoot walked-up game with a ten-bore muzzle-loading hammer gun. This was great fun, but I needed a very steady gun dog with me. When it flushed a pheasant while I was walking through a turnip field, I would lift my gun, swing onto the bird and pull the trigger. After a short delay there would be a thundering boom, followed by a cloud of smoke from the end of the gun barrel, which then took a few seconds to clear. While I could normally see if I had shot the pheasant before the smoke appeared, I still needed my dog to stand by my side waiting for instructions. This is where you need a really good steady dog, because the whole walking-up line had to pause while I reloaded my old gun before walking on again towards the spot where the shot bird had fallen and retrieving it. It takes a few moments to reload a muzzle-loading shotgun with gunpowder, a wad, shot and another wad – all separately packed down with the ramrod – and if my dog wasn't steady and obedient it could dash on in front among the turnips to look for the shot bird, and in the process flush all the unshot birds sitting there.

I shot with this muzzle-loader at various rough shoots with friends who were very patient to wait for me to reload it when we were walking up. It was great fun, and my dog also got used to me shooting with this gun, although it often looked at me when I was reloading, as if asking what the hold up was.

A farmer friend of mine and I proofed and patterned this old gun, and this is how we did it. In the farm stack yard we put a board up some 30 yards, or 27 metres, away, with a 30-inch circle drawn on a bit of white paper stuck onto it. Then we started with a light charge of black gunpowder, followed by wadding and lead shot, packing it all tight into the barrel with the ramrod. We then laid the loaded gun on an old tractor tyre and then tied a bit of string about 4 metres long to the trigger. I then cocked the gun and put a percussion cap on the nipple.

At this point my friend and I retired to the end of the string, and I pulled the trigger-string. After a brief delay there was a thundering boom followed by a cloud of smoke from the gun barrel.

We then went and had a look at the shot pattern on the paper fixed to the board. We kept adjusting the amounts of gunpowder and shot and altering the thickness of the cardboard wads and the felt wads until we had all the shot pattern striking within the 30-inch paper circle on the board. Then we knew the gun would kill game or ground game at 30-odd metres using a load of 2¾ drams of No. 2 fine black gunpowder and 1¼ ounces of No. 6 shot, with cardboard wads 4mm thick and felt wads 1cm thick.

I first measured the black gunpowder into the gun barrel from my powder flask, I then put the cardboard wad in the barrel, which I had cut with a punch, before packing them both down with the ramrod. I then put in the felt wad (cut from carpet felt).

I used to mix two-thirds animal fat (that you can buy from any butcher), and one-third vegetable oil. I dipped the sides only of the felt wads into the melted mixture with a pair of tongs or something similar. This gave me a tighter packed charge, and I got a good shot pattern.

Then I measured the shot into the barrel from my leather shot flask, put in another cardboard wad to hold it and packed everything tight with the ramrod. I was then ready to put the copper ignition cap onto the gun nipple that the hammer would drop onto. After that I just had to cock the gun and I was ready to shoot.

The more I shot with this old muzzle-loader the quicker I got at reloading it.

When my farmer friend and I had established the charge for the gun, I asked him, 'Do you think this gun is now safe to shoot game birds and ground game with?' After a bit of a chat we decided to test (or proof) it by doubling the charge and firing the gun three times with this heavy charge; if there were any weaknesses in the gun barrel this might burst it. Once the barrel had withstood such overpressure, we felt sure that it was safe to shoot with.

It took my farmer friend and I a few weekends to get this shot pattern right with this muzzle-loader, and thereafter I used the shot load and powder charge we had established. I could, however, alter the pattern by adding a cardboard wad after the felt wad: this tends to open up the pattern and spread the shot wider. I discovered this one day when shooting driven pheasants with friends on the Scottish border. I was shooting crossing birds quite well and bringing a few of them down, but I just couldn't seem to get onto the birds coming straight over my head. As these high, fast-flying pheasants kept going overhead and I wasn't hitting any of them, my dog kept looking at me as if asking what the hell I was doing.

I decided to put another cardboard wad in after the felt wad to see what happened. (I knew I shouldn't do this, because I didn't know what would happen, but I tried it anyway.) The apparent result was that I managed to bring down a few of these high overhead birds, and my dog seemed pleased that it was now getting some work to do.

The next weekend I went to tell my farmer friend how I had changed the loading procedure, and we tested the gun on the board in the stack yard, using the extra cardboard wad I had put into the charge after the felt wad. Sure enough, it altered the pattern of the shot, increasing its spread beyond the 30-inch circle – and that was why I had been hitting a few of those high pheasants.

My friend and I agreed there and then that I would never again alter the shotgun charge without first going back to the board. The reason why I had been missing those high, fast, over-head pheasants was simply that I hadn't been giving them a big enough lead to compensate for delay before the slow-igniting black powder exploded with its thundering boom and the cloud of smoke from the gun barrel. In truth, I had been missing those high pheasants because they were too good for me, and even my dog was telling me so.

My dog at that time was a springer spaniel called Patch, who was a great gun dog. To read what he was trying to tell me while we were working in the field was absolutely brilliant. Following the dog's signals made me really sharp and I never knew him to be wrong in what he was trying to tell me.

Some Saturday afternoons a few farmer friends and I used to have a walk over their farms with our guns and dogs. We never shot very much, maybe three or four pheasants, a rabbit or two and a few woodpigeon, but it was always great fun and great company. We might come back to the farm soaking wet from head to toe and with very little in the game bag, but we would all agree we had had a great afternoon. You don't need to shoot a great bag of game to enjoy yourself when you are out with your friends and dogs – and to see good gun dogs at work has always given me great pleasure.

On these friendly walks over the farms we were never in any hurry, and this was ideal for me when I was shooting with my muzzle-loader. On my friend's farm there was an old railway line over 2 miles long, and this was ideal for working gun dogs. I first used to work my gun dog along one side of the line. This was great for the dog, as in places there was quite a lot of undergrowth and shrubs that sometimes held quite a few pheasants and rabbits. On one such Saturday afternoon I had a dog called Percy with me. Percy was always working and hunting in top gear, and I had to fully concentrate on the dog to read what he was trying to tell me while he was hunting. We were walking along the old railway line, and Percy was hunting along the left-hand side when a cock pheasant lifted from the right-hand side of the line and flew across in front of me some 25 metres or so away. I lifted my gun and swung across the pheasant, pulled the trigger and saw it dropping over the railway edge before the cloud of smoke from my gun barrel obscured the view. I turned and looked at Percy, who had stopped when I fired the shot. He looked first at me and then at where the pheasant fell, and he did this two or three times; he was asking me if he should go and get it. When I told him to do so he was off like a shot to retrieve the pheasant while I started to recharge my old gun. When he returned with the cock pheasant he was as pleased as Punch, wagging his tail and emanating pleasure. I patted his head as I took the pheasant from his mouth and told him to sit while I finished reloading my gun. He sat obediently at my side, but kept looking at me and at the railway embankment wondering what the hell we were waiting for and itching to get hunting again.

This gun dog was as good as you could get for working in the field. He was one of the nearest to ideal of the dogs I have had, though not perfect. I haven't seen a perfect gun dog so far; all animals have different faults and peculiarities – that's what makes them so interesting.

Some gun dogs' signals are not all that easy to pick up unless you are with the dog a lot and it is close at hand. Some dogs give quick, short signals, other dogs will make a signal and wait, looking at their master. And some will give a signal to their master and then go ahead and act. In such cases, if the master is not close enough to pick up the dog's signal, he may think the dog is just being stupid. But it is not the dog being stupid but the master for not being in a position to pick up what the dog is trying to convey, or maybe because the dog is being allowed to range too far out in front.

When you train a young dog to work in the field among game birds or ground game (or even if the dog is just a family pet) you want it to be obedient – and obedience is more than simply a matter of making the dog sit, come to heel and stay when instructed. If you have a very strong-willed dog, it can be very difficult for the dog to follow your commands. I have trained all types of gun dogs, and a very wilful spaniel, for instance, can be a great challenge; you have to be a strong person to be able to get the best out of a dog like this and train it successfully.

You have to be unwaveringly consistent and firm with it, as dogs like this will soon pick up any weakness they see in their master and take all possible advantage of it. If you are strong enough to be able to handle such a dog, though, what great pleasure you will get from it!

I always try and get inside a young dog's mind, to find out how it will communicate with me when we are working in the field together. But you can't get this information unless your training is conducted at close quarters.

You can use a sacking training dummy or a ball or a dried hare skin wrapped round a bit of broom handle. You can get a hare skin from a game dealer, or your local butcher may get you one, and tack it to a bit of wood or plywood to dry for a few weeks. Then cut off a bit of broom handle about a foot long, wrap the hare skin round it and tie it very tight with string. If the broom handle is cut much longer than a foot, the dog will be inclined to pick up the dummy near the end, and the other end will then trail on the ground and get dirty. (The idea is to get the dog to pick up dead game by the middle, so that it doesn't get them wet and muddy.)

Make the dog sit beside you, then put one dummy out 2 or 3 metres in front of you, and see how the dog reacts to this.

Make sure the dog doesn't run in and grab the dummy. If it does, bring the dog back and make it sit again until you tell it to move.

When you are training a young gun dog with dummies watch it very carefully. Watch its eyes, its tail, its feet and legs, and its body movements. Then you will begin to understand your dog's behaviour. Even so, it takes time to pick up the dog signals, as you have to learn from the dog, just as the dog has to learn from you what it has to do.

However, you shouldn't need to teach a gun dog how to hunt. This should come naturally to it, with the master just needing to control the dog, and where and when it hunts.

Some gun dogs will look up, though, while others don't know how to. (All dogs will know how to look down: it's just a matter of dropping its head, which comes naturally.) I once had and trained a dog that was very good at looking up;

even when I was shooting woodpigeon and crows on the farm this dog could see the birds coming before I did.

One Saturday I was shooting pheasants with friends in Ayrshire, and at one of the drives a pheasant came flying right across the line of guns, quite some distance out in front. It was making for a small plantation which had some scrub and small bushes in it. The second-to-last gun in the line hit the bird with his second shot, but it still flew on, and it took the last gun in the line to bring it down with his second shot.

I saw the pheasant drop dead in the small plantation, but we were going to walk through this on the next drive, and I thought the dogs would pick the bird up easily. The plantation was about two hundred metres long and about a hundred metres wide, and as we started walking through it a few pheasants were flushed and were shot and picked up. When we got to the end we had picked up eight birds. Then the gun that had shot the crossing pheasant from the previous drive, which had dropped in the plantation, asked if anyone had picked it. No one had, but the landowner said that as we were going back through the plantation to get to the next drive, we would have a look for the dead pheasant on the way.

I was asked to work my dog back along the edge of the left-hand side of the plantation, and when the dog and I got near the end, where I had seen the bird fall, I kept watching the dog and talking to it, encouraging it. All the guns and dogs were now near the end of the plantation hunting for the dead pheasant.

I kept looking and watching my dog, when suddenly it stopped and looked up, then looked at me, then looked at this silver birch tree. I said to the dog, 'Is the pheasant here somewhere?' It looked at me again, then looked up again at this old, broken-down silver birch tree and wagged its tail two or three times.

I called to the other guns and dogs that the pheasant was here somewhere, and we all gathered around. They asked where the pheasant was, and I explained that the dog was telling me it was somewhere around this old half-broken-down silver birch tree. We all looked up the tree, and around it on the ground, but couldn't see anything – and yet the dog still kept telling me the dead bird was here. Now this silver birch tree had partly blown over, the trunk had half snapped about three metres from the ground and twisted as it fell, and it was rotten and partly hollow inside.

When the dead pheasant fell, it had hit the

tree and fallen into the hollow in the trunk, which was why we couldn't see it. One of the guns got a leg up to check the twisted, broken part of the tree, and there was the pheasant, stuck in the hollow.

Two or three of the other guns with dogs looked at me and asked how I knew where the pheasant was. I said the dog had told me the pheasant was around or up the tree somewhere, but one of the guns looked at me again and said, 'Don't be so bloody stupid, Hunter. How the hell could the dog tell you where the dead bird was?'

I thought for a few moments and, as politely as I could, replied that my dog's body language told me the dead pheasant was close at hand, as it kept looking up the tree and then looking at me and wagging its tail.

Nothing more was said at the time, but during our lunch break in the barn the matter came up again, and the dog men asked me if they could train their dogs to talk to them. I told them I hadn't trained my dog to talk to me; I had watched and studied the dog's behaviour and I had used this information to interpret what the dog was experiencing.

I suggested that they should watch their dogs, and they might see them giving signals of what lay ahead – and by studying these signals they would enjoy working and playing with their gun dogs much more.

Dog-owners very often ask me how I get my dog to do this or that so easily, adding that they wish they had a dog like mine. My reply is that you need to enjoy working and playing with your dogs, whether they are gun dogs or household pets. My gun dogs are normally with me or my wife Kathleen all the time, and we train them to fit in with us and do what they are told. Out of this relationship grows an understanding of the individual dog and the ability to interpret and understand its body language that can sometimes be so important.

On one occasion a landowner friend of mine, who had eight paying guests coming for a day's pheasant shooting, asked me to come along and do a bit of picking up and help at the shoot where I could. The party was from an engineering firm that was giving its managers and senior staff a day's pheasant shooting in recognition of the good work they had done for the company. They were staying in a local hotel and my friend asked me to have lunch with them and also stay for dinner in the evening.

There was an elderly gentleman, Mr Wilson, who seemed to be the most senior person in the party, and my friend asked me to look after him and pick up his birds.

It was a very nice friendly party, and the first two pheasant drives in the morning went well. At the third drive three or four pheasants came over this gentleman. He had a go at the first pheasant and just clipped it, but it flew on. Then he swung onto a high hen pheasant and had two shots at it; the bird then took a steep dip as it glided to the ground among some scrub.

At the end of the drive the gentleman suggested we should go and pick up the hen pheasant he had shot, and he asked if I thought my dog would pick it.

I said it would if the bird was dead on the ground. (In fact, I was pretty sure the pheasant wasn't hit but had just been gliding down to land.)

We both went over to where he said the hen pheasant had dropped, and I said to my dog, 'Is there a pheasant lying around?' The dog wasn't a bit interested; it just looked at me as if it were bored.

Mr Wilson looked at me and said, 'Is your dog not going to hunt for my pheasant? Is the dog any bloody good?'

I thought for a few moments, as answering the question he asked required a bit of tact, and I didn't want to upset one of my friend's guests, who I could see wasn't very pleased with me and my dog.

Meanwhile Mr Wilson was getting a bit agitated, and started looking for the pheasant himself, saying that he was pretty sure he had shot the pheasant and it was dead – but my dog just wasn't interested. When Mr Wilson eventually stopped looking for it I said to him tactfully, 'Mr Wilson, you may have clipped the pheasant, but as it took a steep dip and started to glide it could be in the next county.'

'Do you think so?' he replied in a sharp voice, 'I don't!'

Then we all went for lunch in the farm barn, where I had a bit of time to have a chat with some of the other members of the shooting party. Mr Wilson sat beside my friend while they ate.

The afternoon's shooting started off very well. Then Mr Wilson shot a hen pheasant and wounded it. The bird fell to earth but picked itself up and started running towards the guns. It didn't get very far before it saw the next gun about twenty metres away, turned and headed back towards us, and then hid.

When we finished the drive Mr Wilson asked if I thought we would pick that runner, and I said I hoped so. My dog had even marked where the pheasant had fallen to the ground, so I told it to find the bird, and it started to follow the scent trail, with Mr Wilson and myself coming along behind. It tracked the runner for a bit and then the dog sort of stopped and turned back. By then some of the other guns were with us.

I kept following the dog and encouraging it to find the pheasant. After turning back for a few metres, it stopped again and started to wag its tail at me. I looked at Mr Wilson and told him, 'Your pheasant is around here somewhere.'

The dog then put its nose into an old stone land drain that was fairly dry at the time, then looked at me and wagged its tail again. I got down on my knees, put my arm in the drain right up to my shoulder and pulled the pheasant out, still alive.

After dinner in the hotel that night Mr Wilson came over to me and said, 'Sorry I was a bit short with you this morning over my hen pheasant. I hear you are very good with gun dogs, and you have certainly proved that to us today.'

He then shook my hand and said the party had greatly enjoyed their day's shooting and thanked me very much for my help as he handed me an envelope with £50 in it.

3

A Sportsman and His Dog

There's no need for me to give advice on whether you should have any particular breed of gun dog. We all keep the breeds of gun dog we like – and why not? My family have always kept springer spaniels, Labradors, terriers and collies. We've had spaniels and Labradors as working gun dogs, but not for any particular reason beyond the fact that these aren't great big dogs, and we are used to our dogs running in and out of the house. We bred most of our own gun dogs and bought in the odd gun dog puppy from time to time from different breeders or from people who bred dogs that we liked.

It really all depends on what kind of hunting you want your gun dog to do, and whether you like a big breed or a smaller one. For instance, some sportsmen prefer the curly or heavy-coated retriever dogs to the various breeds of springer spaniel or the various types of Labrador.

Bigger breeds, such as pointers and setters, are used a lot in the rugged parts of Scotland, from parts of the West Highlands and Speyside up to Sutherland and Caithness, where they still shoot walked-up grouse over dogs: a charming sport to watch and take part in. Elsewhere the chocolate-coloured breed of Labrador seems to be a great favourite among some game shooters, and is very popular with the general public. Their colour does have a certain charm.

When I am out at various game shoots in the north and on the Scottish Border I see all breeds of gun dogs at work – pointers, setters, Labradors, springer spaniels, retrievers and various long- and short-haired gun dogs – and it is great to see them all. However, I have noticed that by the end of a very wet muddy day some of the bigger and longer-haired breeds come in from the field in a pretty messy state, and can take some cleaning.

Mind you, my own spaniels and Labradors can also come home rather bedraggled, very often in a real mess with muddy feet, belly and tail, and I often need to rinse them off under a hosepipe before drying them with a towel. Gun dogs of all sizes ignore the weather when they are working in the field among game birds and ground game, and it's their masters that have to clean them at the end of the day when they get filthy and wet.

But when you breed gun dogs or buy a puppy from a breeder you never think about what it will be like when it comes home wet and muddy: it's the dog that matters. The most popular breed is probably the Labrador; it is just a good size, not too big and not too small, and it is the breed of gun dog I see most at the various game shoots I go to.

Whatever breed of gun dog you decide to have, though, go and see a good breeder or a good kennels that breeds the type of dog that you prefer. There is no reason why you shouldn't have a dog that is both good-looking and a good worker, though the build of the dog should be suitable for the work it has to do.

Talking of good build and conformation, I well remember a friend of our family asking my father if we could look after her young springer spaniel (a present from a friend that she was going to bring up as a house pet) while she went into hospital for a serious operation from which it would take her several weeks to recover.

She and the young spaniel lived in a cottage in the village and became quite friendly with my parents more or less through her interest in the countryside and farming.

The day before the lady was going into hospital she brought the young dog up to the farm. He was called Tip; he was just over a year old, and the lady said he had a very good nature. The first thing I noticed about him was that his front feet were splayed quite badly, though I didn't say anything to the lady about this. After the lady had gone home, I asked my father to look at Tip's splayed feet, and he said he had seen dogs like that before.

I had my own springer at the time: Bob, who was liver-and-white and just over four years old. My father had bred him, and I had taken him on to train when he was just a puppy.

I put Tip in his own bed in the farmhouse back kitchen beside Bob's bed. (The dogs' beds were just bits of sacking and were often washed when they got dirty.) So the two dogs slept beside one another, were fed at the same time (also beside one another), and they got on very well together, even though they were both males.

When I had Bob out for a refresher training session, or just for a walk, Tip just started to follow us. Then, one Saturday morning when I was out with Bob for a training session, I noticed that when I gave him one chirp on the whistle to stop him, Tip stopped as well. When I gave Bob two chirps on the whistle to bring him to heel,

Tip also came to heel. So I cast Bob out to the left so far and stopped him, and Tip followed Bob and stopped as well. I then signalled Bob to come right across the front of me and cast him to the right so far and stopped him, so that he was practising quartering the ground in front of me. To my amazement, Tip was following Bob and was also working to my instructions.

I carried on this training with both dogs for several weeks before one day suggesting to my father that he come and watch them at a training session. My father was quite impressed with young Tip the dog and his response to my whistle instructions, and he recommended that I take Tip out for a few training sessions on his own to see how he got on.

The next week I took both dogs out for separate training sessions. During his sessions, Tip was at first looking to see where Bob was, but then I whistled him to stop, which he did. After that I let him run around for a bit, before whistling him to come to heel, which he did straight away, and I made a fuss of him for being so good.

Because of his splayed front feet, Tip was very different from our other dogs, and we would normally have ruled out having him as a working dog. Because of this I didn't push him too hard at the first few dog training sessions I had with him alone, although I did want to see what he was made of.

I used dummies a little bit, and he seemed to be shaping up and was very keen. Because of his splayed feet he wasn't as quick at getting around as Bob was, but I could see he would make a useful gun dog for certain types of shooting, and he had a lovely nature.

Back then we used to grow a field or two of oats as feed for the farm's horses, chickens, ducks and geese, and a field or two of beans and oats mixed which we crushed for the dairy cows and for the young dairy stock. We cut the corn and beans with a binder, which tied the stems into sheaves, and then we stood four sheaves together with the heads upright to make a stook – this was to get the heads ripe and dry before we took in the sheaves.

But this ripening and drying could take several weeks, if the weather didn't co-operate, and during that time the woodpigeons used to come and sit on the stook heads and eat the corn and beans. They could make a real mess, what with the amount they ate and the droppings they left behind, if we didn't take steps to try and stop them by shooting the woodpigeons.

So when I went pigeon-shooting in the cornfield I used to take Tip with me, and he was very good at retrieving a few shot pigeons until he got his mouth full of feathers, when I had to clean his mouth out. (The trouble with woodpigeon feathers is when a gun dog gets a mouthful of the feathers, and they get wet with the saliva, they stick in the mouth and the dog sometimes shakes its head to try and clear them.)

Sometimes I would build a hide of corn sheaves and wait for the pigeons to fly over the field before landing on the stooks. I used to sit in the hide on a drum or anything that was lying around, like a bit of tree branch, and shoot the woodpigeons from the hide. Tip used to sit in the hide with me and watch them until I sent him out to pick the shot birds.

I have shot hundreds of woodpigeons from our oats, beans and barley fields over the years. When a flock of hungry woodpigeons descend onto a crop, especially when parts of the crop has been fattened by the weather, the pigeons can eat a lot of the grain and beans and do a lot of crop damage.

Alongside the pigeon-shooting I carried on giving Tip some training sessions on his own with the dried hare-skin dummies. Although he was shorter than Bob, he was turning into a strong dog and was always willing to hunt and work. After we had had him for about three months, his lady owner, now home but still recovering from her stomach operation, contacted my father and asked him if he would continue looking after Tip until she had fully recovered. My father asked me if I was quite happy looking after Tip, and I said I was. I suggested to my father that we could use Tip during the shooting season and give him some experience.

When the shooting season started I took Tip along to shoot flighting duck in the early evening on the marsh, where there was a fairly big pool of water surrounded by some silver birch trees, rushes, shrubs and boggy ground. The marsh was a good place for a great variety of wildlife and wildfowl of all species, and it was little disturbed apart from our few nights' duck shooting and a few days' pheasant shooting.

Tip and I went into a hide I had previously cut into a rhododendron bush beside the water, from where we could look right across the water and the marsh. I had been feeding the ducks with a few crushed oats at the water edge near this hide.

I didn't know how well Tip would do at retrieving in fairly deep water, but it wasn't very long before I found out. A pair of mallard came flying right across in front of me, and I shot them both with a right and left. They dropped into the water some twenty metres from my hide, so I sent Tip out to fetch the ducks. He had marked where both ducks had fallen, and he leapt straight into the water and swam out to the nearest duck, gently got hold of it and swam back to me with it in his mouth.

I took the bird from him and sent him back for the second one; again he went straight out into the water and brought it back. This was a really great display of retrieving ducks from the water, especially since it was Tip's first time duck shooting.

I shot another six mallard that evening, and Tip retrieved them all for me, some from the water and some from the scrub beside the water – a good evening's work for a young dog, all the more so because two of them had to be retrieved in the dark.

The next morning I told my father how well Tip had done at the flighting duck, and he suggested I bring Tip along to our first pheasant shoot to see how he stood up to the hard work of hunting. I did so, and worked Tip hard during the morning, then I looked at his splayed feet at lunchtime and found them red and sore from hunting through the thick, rough woodland, so I left him at home in the afternoon.

I really enjoyed hunting and working both Tip and Bob that season, but then disaster struck Tip. Near the end of the season we had a mid-week shoot, as there were plenty of pheasants around, and Bob and Tip worked very hard all morning, as all the dogs did. In the mid afternoon we were all walking from one drive to the next when we came to a stone wall, which was quite high on the side from which we approached it. Some of the gun dogs were up and over the wall into the next field straight away but we walked along the wall to an iron gate with some sheep netting on the bottom half, to stop sheep getting from one pasture to another. The gate was well tied up, so my friends and I had to climb over it into the next field, and most of the gun dogs were already over the wall.

When my friends and I climbed over the gate, though, I couldn't see Tip. I went and looked over the wall, and there he was, struggling to climb up the wall but unable to get over; he had obviously tried several times, because he was puffing and panting. As he tried again I bent over the wall top and caught him by the scruff of the neck and pulled him over the wall top.

As the group of us moved on I noticed Tip just wasn't right; when I called him he just looked up at me. And when we got to the next drive he didn't want to work: he just lay down. I called on my father to come and have a look at him, and my father said Tip had pulled something and told me to put him on the trailer and take him home (we had a tractor and trailer with us at the shoots to transport our guests around).

I quickly picked Tip up and put him in the trailer among some straw bales to keep him comfortable and drove off for home. There I lifted Tip off the trailer, carried him into the farm kitchen and put him on his bed; he didn't look too good, but unfortunately I had to take the tractor and trailer back and push on to catch up with the other guns.

When we got home at the end of the day I dashed in to see how Tip was. He wasn't very well at all; he had been sick and was trying to vomit up some more fluid. I wrapped him up with his bedding and went back to join our shooting friends who by then were in the farm-house having drinks. I didn't say anything to them at the time about Tip. Then, after our friends had all eaten and gone home, I asked my father to come and have a look at Tip, and I told him he had been sick and was vomiting up fluid.

My father had a good look at Tip, examining the dog and pressing him here and there, but Tip wasn't bothered; he just lay there.

After a few moments my father said to me he was pretty sure Tip had strained his heart muscle, and that was what was making him vomit. He must have done it when he was trying to climb the stone wall; he would have tried a number of times to get up and over, but because of his splayed front feet he would have found it very difficult trying to climb up the wall and this is when he will have pulled a muscle.

My father said Tip was finished, and for the next few days he didn't eat or drink anything but kept trying to vomit up mucus from his stomach. My father said it would be kindest to put Tip down, as he would be no good as a gun dog any more, and he volunteered to go and see Tip's lady owner and tell her what had happened.

A day or two later Tip was put down, and I buried him in the stack yard beside our other gun dogs and farm dogs.

4

Gun Dog Faults

There are quite a lot of faults with some gun dogs, and a lot of the faults have to do with their breeding. I have come across gun dogs that didn't have the stamina to do a full day's work in the field, dogs with ear problems, dogs with feet problems, dogs with eye problems and dogs with conformation problems. There seems to be a tendency among some breeders to breed dogs for the show bench. That is because, if your dog wins at some of the top dog shows in the country, then you have a dog that's worth a lot of money, and so is any of its offspring. This is a way for breeders to make names for themselves.

When you go and buy a gun dog puppy from a breeder ask if its parents have any faults, or if there are any faults with this strain of gun dog. What you see with a gun dog puppy is not always what you get, so dig deep and ask questions before you hand over the cash, even if you like the look of the dog very much. Remember you could be working in the field with the dog for the next ten years or more.

The most common fault in working gun dogs that I have come across in the field is that most dogs are not disciplined enough, and are inclined to hunt and chase for their own pleasure. Preventing or correcting this begins at home, because management of dogs around the house and kennels relates directly to the dog's behaviour when working in the field. If you can't control and handle gun dogs around the house and kennels, then there is very little chance indeed of your controlling them in the field, when they are out working among game as they are bred to do.

Gun dogs resemble children in many ways. They are very quick to gauge the character of whoever is in charge of them, and will seek to take liberties whenever possible. Both children and dogs thrive on discipline, consistency and knowing the boundaries of acceptable behaviour: qualities that are often in short supply today.

A young, highly excitable gun dog at a driven pheasant shoot may see its master shoot a few birds that drop close at hand, and sometimes it may lose all self-control and run in to retrieve one of them without being told to. He knows he will be punished for his wrongdoing but may be determined to have his fling before he returns to good behaviour and his punishment. But escape his punishment he must not.

Very often young gun dogs with such a very strong temperament end up making the best gun dogs, provided you can handle them. A timid, docile gun dog that never does anything wrong will very seldom be worth its keep. It may be quite good retrieving shot game birds which are easily seen, and which you could quite easily pick up yourself, but when it comes to hunting down a wounded game bird that has crossed a small stream and has travelled several hundred metres away, such a dog immediately gives up and looks to his master for guidance.

Training and working with gun dogs is not easy – and indeed many gun dog owners really ought to be trained themselves before they start on their dogs. Some breeds of gun dog are easier to train than others: some Labradors may need less training than, say, a very strong-headed springer spaniel. My father used to tell us that one should train Labradors for several years before taking on a springer spaniel with a strong temperament.

A big mistake that many people make with a young gun dog is that, when they are exercising it in a lane, wood or park, they let it run too far out in front of them. To my mind, avoiding this is the secret of gun dog training and getting control of your dog. Ranging too widely makes training more difficult, so keep turning the dog back when it's about thirty metres out (it still has plenty of scope for play and exercise within that range). I know some busy people have little time to spend with their dogs during the week, but if their partners take the dog out for a daily run it is very important that they, too, keep turning the dog back. In time the dog will start looking back and turning itself.

If anyone is thinking of taking a young gun dog with them on a pheasant shoot, I would advise them not to unless they can stop the dog and call it back to heel, preferably with a dog whistle, or unless they are prepared to keep the dog on a bit of rope all day and simply let it see what goes on at a pheasant shoot, rather than try to work it. Many people training gun dogs go about it the wrong way. If the young dog likes water, or has a good nose, or retrieves well, they concentrate on these good points. But all these good points can be developed later, after the dog has been brought under reliable control. Unless you have full control of a young dog by the time it is six months to a year old, then you will have a very difficult job on your hands ultimately to train the dog to a fairly high standard. Even gun dogs that are supposed to be well trained (including my own) can let you down when you least expect it. When you work with gun dogs or domestic animals the unexpected is always just around the corner no matter how well you think you know them.

I was once out on a walked-up pheasant shoot in Cumberland shooting over dogs. We were a party of eight guns, with five gun dogs between us, and two of them were guests, with dogs that I didn't know. I had a Labrador bitch called Sheila with me, a dog I had trained myself from a puppy and was always proud to take to any shoot, as I knew she was very sound and thought she would never let me down. (I never had any need to peg her down at any shoot, as she was always just hanging around me or standing at my heels.)

We had a really good morning walking up pheasants in small woods and along rough bank sides and through scrub areas of marshland. We each carried our own lunch in our game bags, and around 12.30 we decided to stop for lunch, and as it was a very nice day we decided to sit behind a stone wall at the end of a field over-looking the neighbouring farmer's land.

We were all enjoying our lunch, with the dogs sitting looking at us to see if they could cadge bits of our food, when suddenly a hare came trotting around the end of the field right in front of us. When it saw us, it stopped, took one look at us and then dashed off towards the neighbour's land. One of our dogs broke ranks and started to chase after the hare, and in a few split seconds all the dogs followed suit, including my dog Sheila. Then, of course, all the shooters started whistling, bawling, shouting and swearing at their dogs to Bloody Well Get Back Here!

The neighbour had sheep in the field, sheep that were due to lamb in a few weeks' time, and the hare ran right in among them, with the dogs in hot pursuit, scattering them in all directions. One of the dogs kept barking as the chase continued, which made the sheep still more panic-stricken – and my dog Sheila was also in there helping the havoc along! Two of the dog-owners were also in the field, running after their dogs and swearing and shouting at them.

As quickly as the commotion had started, it was all over again: the hare slipped through a gap in the far hedge and disappeared; the dogs all looked stunned at its disappearance; and the sheep just stood and looked around them. Because of the barking and shouting the farmer came out to see what was going on, but by the time he reached the field he was too late to see the sheep being scattered by the dogs. Moreover, the two dog men had by then caught their dogs. They walked over to the farmer to tell him what had happened and apologize for their dogs getting in among his sheep. Of course, the farmer wasn't all that pleased at seeing so many dogs among his sheep, but the dogs weren't interested in the sheep, and he could see they had come to no harm. So, after a few more words with the farmer, the two dog owners made their exit from the field.

The other dogs had come trotting back to where we were sitting having our lunch. My dog Sheila came back with her tail between her legs and sat down at my feet, knowing very well she had done wrong. I ticked her off very savagely, regarding that as sufficient punishment for her misdemeanour. (If she had attempted to attack the sheep, however, that would have been a very different matter, and she would have been severely punished.) I also apologized for my dog's behaviour to my landowner friend who had asked me to his shoot. He told me not to worry about it; he would see his neighbour, the sheep farmer, and put the matter right.

But why was it we were all so concerned that

our dogs had run in when there were sheep about? Why did we take it so seriously? Well, dogs chasing sheep is potentially very serious indeed. There are many people from the towns and cities who come into the countryside to enjoy the sport of game shooting, and many of them have gun dogs. But whereas to them the countryside is a place for field sports, for farmers and landowners it's their workplace – the place where they make their living. They keep and breed a great variety of domestic animals, poultry, vegetables, cereals and fish: top-quality food for the general public to eat.

Among the animals, sheep are one of the most important, because they can thrive on the poor grazing of upland country at altitudes of up to 3,000 feet above sea level, producing excellent meat, as well as wool and milk (for cheese). Sheep of nearly sixty different breeds can be found on farms throughout the country, with some breeds linked to certain districts (Herdwicks, for instance: a very hardy breed found in the English Lake District, probably of Scandinavian origin). But the most common upland sheep are the blackface breeds, which have also spread all over the world where conditions are hard.

Throughout the British countryside there is

At the end of a
pheasant drive

Game shooters
discussing the
next pheasant
drive

Labrador gun
dogs are a
favourite with
game shooters

The author using two dried hare skins to train a springer spaniel

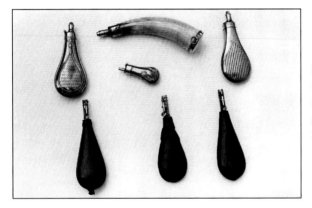

Some of the author's shot and gunpowder flasks

The author training a gun dog in a turnip field

A spaniel being trained. Note how the dog has lifted one leg

The game shooters at Walby in Cumberland

The author training a gun dog using shot pheasants

Young boys at the end of walking a rough shoot

The author shooting wood pigeons at home in 1963

A wood pigeon feeding in a wheat field. Note the white ring on the bird's neck denoting that it is an adult

A brown hare among some long wet grass

A picture of a young lady at a game shoot in Cumberland with her rough-coated gun dogs

The dog returns with the duck from the pond

The author at the start of the game shooting season in Northumberland

A farmer stops to have a chat with the game shooters

A game shooter waiting for pheasants being flushed over him

The author
talking to his gun
dog at the end of
a pheasant shoot

A cock pheasant.
Note the rich
colours of the
bird

Bill Colclough
with his wife
Pat, and one
of his sons,
Scott, who is
a gamekeeper
on Blanchland
Moor

The gamekeeper discussing the next pheasant drive with the shoot owner at Brackenbank in Cumberland. The author has been a guest at Brackenbank shoot from time to time

The shooter walking through a turnip field

A group of game shooters in Cumberland

The author with one of his gun dogs

Good water-proof clothes are needed when walking a wet game crop

Two different types of shooting jackets

Game shooters heading for lunch at the end of the morning's pheasant shooting

Having refreshments in the shooting hut at the end of the day

The beaters collecting at the end of a pheasant drive

The author with
Melanie and
Mike Douglas
at Wall in
Northumberland

The nest of a hen
pheasant with
fourteen eggs

Walking a
rough shoot

Kathleen, Helen and Richard Adair with a young gun dog at the seaside

A woodcock. Note how well it blends in with its habitat

Walking a rough shoot

The Herdwick sheep. A small, hardy breed found in the Lake District

Training young gun dogs on the moors to flush rabbits

A young red grouse taking cover on the moor

Bill and Pat Colclough with the author at Penny Pie in Blanchland, Co. Durham

A black grouse at dawn in the spring. Males (blackcocks) congregate on display grounds, known as a lek

Wild goats in the Galloway hills and moors in Scotland

Young pheasant
chicks in an
open pen, being
checked over by
the gamekeeper

Gun dogs being
kept in a wire
pen, so they can
see what's going
on around them

Shot pheasants
being checked
in the game
larder by the
gamekeeper

The Gibson family, from the North. They are farmers and game-shooters, pictured here with two of their gun dogs and two working collies

A curlew, sitting on four eggs on the moor

The Labrador retrieving a rabbit

the problem that many sheep and lambs are attacked and killed by dogs every year, and it is a problem that doesn't seem to be getting any better. In the spring dogs can cause a lot of damage to sheep flocks if they attack ewes that are due to lamb; such attacks can cause the ewes to abort their lambs.

Dogs may legally be (and sometimes are) shot when caught in the act of worrying, chasing or attacking sheep. On the other hand, a sheep farmer or his shepherd has no legal right to shoot a stray dog found wandering about in a field where there are sheep. (Neither has a landowner or his gamekeeper any legal right to shoot a stray dog wandering in a wood where they keep pheasants.)

But you will probably have noticed that when you come across some sheep in a field, they are inclined to run away for a few metres, then stop and look back to see what they are running from (rabbits also have the same tendency). It is this running away that sets the dogs off chasing after them. So, when dogs chase and worry sheep, it's not the dog's fault for following a natural inclination that needs to be controlled; it's the owners' fault for not keeping their dogs under control. And the consequences can be fatal, whether for the sheep or the dogs.

So how do you train your dog not to chase sheep? Firstly pick a field where there is a public footpath and there are sheep in the field. Put your dog on a short leash and try to get as close to the sheep as you can without going off the footpath. When you are close to the sheep give a strong backward pull on the leash and say 'No' to your dog in a firm voice. In time it should get to know not to chase the sheep, and then you can extend its leash, before eventually you are able to let your dog off the leash. However, the process will take time, so persevere with this training and take it gradually, and you will score in the end.

Alternatively, when you see sheep in a field there will usually be a farm not too far away that owns the sheep. Go along to the farm with your dog and see the farmer. Tell him you want to train your dog not to chase sheep, and ask if he can help you. Most sheep farmers will be very willing to help and may take you and your dog out among the sheep. If so, keep your dog on the leash and remember: a good strong pull back on the leash, and say 'No' in a very firm manner. It shouldn't take too long before the dog can be let off the leash, and it will just ignore the sheep altogether.

Sometimes, though, you do get the very odd

strong-headed gun dog that just won't listen and will still want to chase the sheep when they run.

AILMENTS

The ears can be a problem at times with long-eared gun dogs such as spaniels. When they are hunting and working in the field at full tilt in long, wet grass and scrubland, if they turn very quickly their ears flip back and drops of water and bits of debris can get into the ear canal and set up an infection in the ear. This is more of a problem when the dogs are out continually hunting and flushing game birds in wet conditions.

When dogs have an ear infection they will often keep shaking their heads. It can be resolved fairly easily with a few ear drops from the vet. You will soon get to know what drugs work best for your dog.

Don't let this put you off buying a springer spaniel, though. They are great dogs to work with and they also make nice family pets.

Eyes, too, can sometimes be a problem with working gun dogs. They sometimes get scratches and scrapes from charging through bramble bushes and rough scrubland while they are working, or a prick from a bush or a cut or a bump that can cause inflammation of the eye.

I check the damage and sometimes find I can just leave the injury to heal by itself. However, if it hasn't shown any signs of healing after a few days, I may then treat the eye injury with a cream or eye drops from the vet.

I have worked with gun dogs all my life and have come across all types of dog injuries. Some, like a cut foot or pad, can on occasion keep a dog from working for a week to ten days while the injury heals. There is nothing worse when it comes to a shooting day than your dog being sick or injured and unable to join you. This is bound to happen when you shoot as much as I do (two or three days a week during the shooting season) unless you have two or three working gun dogs to choose from.

Rheumatism can be another problem for working gun dogs and can slow them down quite a bit. One thinks of rheumatism as coming with old age, but, while there is some truth in this, it is not always true. Young working dogs that get knocked about a bit in the field can develop rheumatism in some joints at quite an early age. As working gun dogs get older, though, they tend to get rheumatism in the back and the hind legs, which seem to give way more easily and are not as steady. However, dogs can still do some field-work with the help of pain-killers, and acupuncture can help some gun dogs.

If working gun dogs get to be about ten years old, are still working in the field and are still fairly fit, then they are doing very well, even if they may have slowed down quite a bit. Keeping a dog's weight down will keep it working longer.

A real scourge to the dog world is distemper, which can be fatal to some dogs if they have not been vaccinated against it. The disease is caused by a virus, and from the early signs and symp-toms it may look as if the dog has a cold, with red runny eyes, a snuffly nose and a temperature.

Distemper crops up from time to time, espe-cially in urban areas. I can well remember it broke out in various parts of the north in the early 1980s, mostly in young, unvaccinated dogs but also in dogs that receive their regular booster vaccination. The disturbing feature of some of these cases was that a high proportion of the dogs appeared to have responded to treat-ment for the early symptoms, but after a few weeks some started having fits; sometimes paralysis occurred and the dogs had to be destroyed.

My advice to all dog-lovers is, if and when you buy a puppy, get it vaccinated and check with the vet what booster vaccinations it will need and when. If you get the dog from a shelter or from kennels, ask if it has been vaccinated and what for.

5

Ducks and Water

If you have a duck pond on your farm or on your estate it is a great pleasure to see a flock of wild duck approach and circle around the pond, and then suddenly drop into it.

For many years I had two duck ponds, both were very different. One was a very early pond, by which I mean that the wild mallard come flocking into the pond from early August and September at the start of the duck shooting season in September. The other one is quite a long pond with a few trees on either side and at each end, making it more difficult to see the wild ducks coming into the pond at dusk. But it is a great pond for working with gun dogs, because they have to find the ducks I shoot, which can be very difficult at dusk.

Working gun dogs at duck shooting has a certain unpredictable charm, for those I have trained and worked with have varied quite a bit when it came to ducks and water. Some dogs are not all that keen on getting into water, while others leap straight in and never think about how deep the pond is or how cold the water.

I have never had a gun dog that simply wouldn't go into water, although with some I have had to spend a lot of time training them to enter it – firstly into shallow water, to give the dog confidence, and then later into deeper water – and this could take quite a while with some of them.

If a gun dog is timid about going into water, it is best to start the dog's training in the summer months, when the water is less cold (or should be).

Start by putting the dog on a lead, walking into a small, shallow burn or stream and then walking up or along the stream with the dog following. Then play with the dog a bit in the shallow water, but keep it on the lead. If the dog likes to play with a ball or a bit of stick, take that into the water with you and get the dog to play with it.

This accustoming to water will not happen overnight but will take time and patience. I sometimes take a young gun dog to the coast and walk it along the edge of the sea on the lead. Be careful, though, not to take the dog too far into the sea to start with, if it doesn't like water. It isn't a good idea just to force a young gun dog into deep water when it doesn't want to go: it will only make it more difficult later to get it to retrieve a shot duck or pheasant that has fallen into a deep pond or river. Patient coaxing works better.

If you use a dried hare-skin as a training dummy or a canvas training dummy, and the dog loves to retrieve it, don't put the dummy in the water at this stage. What you can do, though, if the river or stream is not very wide and only about eight inches (20 cm) deep, is to throw the dummy over onto the dry bank on the far side and walk over the river with the dog on the lead. Then, once the dog is happy with that, send it across the stream by itself to retrieve the dummy. Keep at it, and gradually go into deeper water, until you can just fling the dummy into a deep pond and send the dog in to retrieve it.

If a dog is water shy you will have to work on this and gradually give the dog the confidence it needs to automatically just jump or run into the water to retrieve a shot duck. This can involve a lot of time and patience, but some dogs I have trained would end up prepared to swim the Channel to pick up a shot duck, if they had marked its fall.

One Saturday I was at a friend's rough shoot, with several hundred acres, where I have been going for over thirty years. It's a very friendly shoot, and we always get a very mixed bag of pheasants, rabbits, woodcock, duck, snipe, hares and the odd grouse.

A small river runs through the ground, and a duck or two always gets up there as we walk in line. On this occasion two of the guns in the line were walking along the river bank, where there are lots of trees and bushes, when a duck lifted from the river. As it climbed away one of them shot it, and it fell back down into the river. When I walked over to the riverside with my dog to pick the bird we found it had a trout half-swallowed in its mouth. (Honest! I saw it myself!)

Another weekend I was with a party on the Scottish Border, shooting with my ordinary 12-bore shotgun, and had a very special spaniel called Patch with me. We were a party of twelve guns with about seven gun dogs of various breeds, and again there was a river a few metres wide running through the shoot.

We had just finished a pheasant drive, and the guns were walking in line across two fields to the next pheasant drive, with two of them walking along the riverside, when six mallard lifted from the river. Climbing, they flew out over the fields where some of the other guns were walking, but then saw them and turned back towards the river.

The ducks were turning and heading back for the river. By this time the ducks were quite high, and I thought they were maybe just out of range, but some of the guns were shooting at them, and I did see one falling, though I couldn't see where it actually dropped.

When we got to the end of the field I noted some of the guns making for the riverside to look for the shot duck. The rest of us waited for them by the fence at the end of the field. But after about twenty minutes there was still no sign of the other guns coming from the riverside. My friend the landowner asked me to go and see what the hold-up was and try and find the duck while he and the others moved on.

Another dog man said he would come with me to see if he could help, and we joined the other guns with their dogs at the riverside. We discovered that they had found the duck, but it was stuck in the river and none of the dogs could get it. There had been a lot of rain over the last ten days, so there was a lot of water in the rivers. What happened was that the shot duck had dropped into the fast-flowing river and been washed some way downstream and then lodged between two tree branches sticking up in midstream. None of the dogs could get to it, as there was a small, fast whirlpool of water in front of where the duck was stuck.

When the other dog man and I approached the riverside two of the guns were encouraging their dogs into the fast-flowing water to get the duck, but the dogs weren't having any of it; they were keen enough, but they wouldn't go into the fast current. Two of the other gun dogs kept moving forward to the river edge and then they backed off.

Patch and I both had a quick look at where the duck was trapped; it wasn't going to be easy to get. I asked Patch if he could get the duck, and twice he wagged his tail and looked at me. I knew then that he would get the trapped duck. So he and I went upstream for a few metres, and then I sent him in to get the duck. He jumped straight into the fast-flowing river and got washed down until he was above the whirlpool of water, then he made a great effort to swim behind the whirlpool to get the trapped duck. He grabbed it and then let the whirlpool wash them both back into the current, and finally he was washed several metres downriver with the duck, where I helped him out of the water.

Finding a shot mallard duck at dusk or in the

darkness can be very difficult, even with the best of gun dogs, if the duck is wounded when it drops and it drops on the ground beside the pond. Ducks can crawl and hide in the most unlikely places and stay perfectly still. I sometimes take my dog back to the duck pond the next morning in daylight to try and find a duck that we couldn't find the night before. It is even possible for a duck to have been hit and fall to the ground and then, when having shaken itself, take off again; I have known this happen many times.

A wounded mallard duck can run for quite a distance, and it can hide in a tuft of grass – or in the water at the edge of the pond, with its beak just sticking above the water – and stay very still. It takes a top-quality gun dog to pick up a wounded duck hiding in the edge of a pond like this. When my dog was hunting for a wounded mallard I have sometimes spotted its beak at the side of my duck pond among some long grass. I would then call the dog to heel and tell it to hunt where I saw the duck's head, and if the duck moved the dog would have it – but if the duck stayed still the dog could miss it, for the best of gun dogs can miss a wounded mallard hiding like this.

Hunting for a wounded duck is not a job for a young gun dog learning its craft, nor is it a job for a game shooter with little gun dog experience. When a mallard is shot dead and it drops to the ground or into the water it is normally quite an easy job for a gun dog to pick up the dead bird. But when a duck is shot and winged, and it drops to the ground or into the pond, then it's a different ball game trying to find it and pick it up. A wounded duck can hide in very little cover, lying stretched out with its head down and staying perfectly still for a long time. You really almost have to trample on a wounded duck on the ground before it will move, as I have found out many times over the years.

When a wounded mallard falls into a pond or a river it may hide by sinking its whole body, leaving only its beak above the water so that it can breathe. This way it can fool most game shooters and gun dogs. I have watched a wounded mallard duck stay motionless, with just its beak above water for half an hour or more, until I disturbed it.

Teal are smaller duck than mallard and will come straight into a duck pond or into water like an express train, whereas some mallard will circle a pond several times before they drop into the water. Even if they are getting fed regularly at a pond and have got used to coming into the food, mallards are very wary birds indeed. If they are the least big unsure about something at the pond they will circle it a few times before dropping in to the water.

One evening my father and I, with a dog apiece, were flighting ducks at dusk on our duck pond. It was quite a windy night but dry, and we had shot a few mallard and teal, which the dogs had picked, and I had shot two ducks that had fallen outside the duck pond and that I knew weren't dead.

When we finished shooting we set off to look for them. We had two good gun dogs with us, and we each carried a torch to help find the wounded ducks and to see where we were going in the inky dark.

After about half an hour the dogs had found one of the ducks in among some rushes (there was a lot of water lying around the pond, and the area was marshy with wet bogs). Some twenty minutes after that my father said we would hunt for the duck for another quarter of an hour or so, and if we still couldn't find it, he suggested I should come back first thing in the morning in daylight to try again.

I was standing still flashing my torch around me when my father spoke, and I just happened to look down and there was the wounded mallard, flat out, half covered in water among some wet rushes, lying perfectly still; my left foot was almost touching it.

We have a code of practice among the game shooters that any wounded game bird or ground game are hunted for with gun dogs the same day and picked up if at all possible, no matter how long it takes. I have hunted for hours at game shoots with my gun dogs for the odd wounded pheasant that has run on and hidden some-where.

———◆———

The other day I was asked a very interesting question by two gun dog owners. Can wild ducks smell?

Yes, they appear to have a very keen scent indeed. When I am stalking wild ducks on a river, if I spot some I may need to make a detour to try and approach them from a different angle, so as to get a shot at them as they lift out of the middle of the river. In a case like this I always have to be very careful about crossing the wind if it's blowing towards the ducks, for they will instantly notice my scent and rise when I am a long way off, even though they cannot see or hear me.

And I have noticed many times that when I am approaching one of my duck ponds to feed the ducks, they will rise from the pond long before I get near it – sometimes when I am about fifty metres away. I then stop and notice the wind is blowing from me towards the ducks. Similarly, I have often found while walking the bank of a twisting river with my dog that wild mallard will lift from the river away in front of me, well out of gun range and before I could even see them on the river. Again, I would wonder what had scared them off the river but, when I thought about it, I found I was upwind of the ducks.

Conversely, when feeding the wild ducks on my duck pond, I have often found that if I approach the pond against the wind I can get right up to it, and the ducks don't lift until they see me. And when my dog and I walk a riverbank upwind, and walk into the wind, I can normally get very close to ducks or any other wildlife on the river. Whenever you are trying to get close to any wild birds or animals, the secret is to use the conditions, and in particular the wind.

6

Shooting Protocol and Safety

Game shooting has moved on since the last century when I started going out with my father and friends at the age of about seven. We used to walk up our quarry and shoot it over gun dogs.

It was very hard work.

We used to walk all day carrying a crust of bread and a lump of cheese in our pockets, then sit down behind a hedge or stone wall to eat our lunch. Apart from the long day's walking and game shooting, we also had to carry the game birds, hares and rabbits we shot – if we couldn't leave them somewhere and then pick them up on our way back. We would finish the day with a small bag to show for it, but a great deal of fun and enjoyment from shooting with family friends and neighbours, and because we had walked so much we all ended up exhausted at the end of the day, and so did the gun dogs.

It was at these walking-up shoots that I learnt the skills and crafts of game shooting with gun dogs and the etiquette of shooting. The dogs, too, had to work hard at these shoots, learning and perfecting their skills by working among game birds and ground game, and they were always raring to go and enjoyed hunting and working hard.

At some game shoots today the guns don't have very far to walk, as they are transported around the shoot in motor vehicles or trailers and dropped off as near as possible to where they will stand at a peg and shoot the birds being driven over them by a team of beaters.

Some guns pay a lot of money to shoot hundreds of driven birds in a day. Game shooting is big business today, and there seem to be plenty of people out there wanting to spend their money on it. I meet lots of nice men, boys and women who come game shooting today from all walks of life and from many different countries. Sadly, though, many of them have never had the chance to acquire the skills of the countryside or to understand the game shooting etiquette that goes with the sport. All they want to do is shoot as many game birds as they can in a day and enjoy the social side of the sport.

———•◆•———

When we were walking up on some shoots and shooting over the dogs, there was nearly always someone at the shoot who would be walking a few metres in front of the line of guns, to try and get a better chance of shooting any birds flushed by the dogs ahead by being closer to them. This practice is very bad manners, for the extremely sound reason that it is very dangerous: the gun walking a few metres in front of the line is restricting the field of fire of the guns walking on either side of him, which makes it much more difficult for them to shoot safely and increases his own risk of being shot by mistake. I have been at shoots where the gamekeeper had to keep calling out to guns walking forward to keep in line. And at some such shoots the owner or gamekeeper will tell the guns before the shoot starts to keep in line and not to shoot at any low birds or ground game.

The gamekeeper at a driven pheasant shoot will also often tell the beaters to keep in line and not to miss any birds lying hidden in thick cover or bramble bushes. This is because lots of beaters today at pheasant, partridge or grouse shoots are just young boys and girls who are there for an enjoyable day out and for the money, but who know very little about the etiquette of the sport.

Many shoots nowadays are held on a Saturday

when lots of young people have finished work for the week, and the school week too is finished, so a bit of pocket money (£20 or £30 for a day's beating) is very welcome – but also very well earned, for beating on some shoots is very hard work indeed.

————•◆•————

At some pheasant shoots where there are lots of pheasants in a wood the gun dog men and women in the beating line are instructed by the keeper to keep their dogs back, so that they don't dash forward and flush a large cloud of pheasants forward over the guns all at the same time, because the guns won't be able to deal with them all at once (the aim is to flush the birds more gradually). But it can happen that a dog dashes away forward and causes havoc among the pheasants, perhaps because the dog-handler is inexperienced and has never been to this particular shoot before. If this happens on the first or second drive of the day, the shoot owner or the gamekeeper will have a discreet word with the dog-handler and tell him or her to either keep the dog on a lead or go home. I have heard this remark being made at a number of game shoots about gun dogs.

In such cases the dog-handler shows no respect for the shoot owner and the gamekeeper in letting their dog run forward and flush all the birds at once, because this can spoil the whole day's shooting for everybody, guns and beaters alike. What the handler should do, if they haven't been at the shoot before, is to keep the dog on the lead during the first drive and watch and see what the procedure is at the shoot. They should only let the dog off the lead if they are asked to go and pick someone's shot birds, or to hunt for a wounded pheasant that has run on and hidden somewhere. That way, the dog-handler and the dog will be very much appreciated and they may be asked back to another pheasant shoot in the future.

———•———

There is another breech of shooting etiquette that I have encountered a few times: borrowing cartridges from other guns during the day. When I am invited to a shoot I try and estimate how many cartridges I will need, and then take more than that amount (to allow a margin of error) with me on the day. It is selfish and bad manners to go to a shoot, run out of cartridges during the day and then borrow more off the other people.

At one pheasant shoot I was shooting with a party that included the son of a well-known country family. At the start of the second drive this guy approached me and said, 'Hunter, could I borrow some cartridges from you? I will give you them back at lunchtime.' I had a cartridge bag over my shoulder with fifty cartridges in, a cartridge belt with another twenty-five and about thirty cartridges loose in the pockets of my jacket, so, although it seemed odd that this guy was running short of cartridges even before the second drive, I gave him the benefit of the doubt and handed him thirty cartridges. Nevertheless, I thought it was very bad manners and a very mean trick not to have enough cartridges, though I kept my thoughts to myself, as I didn't want to upset my host, who had asked me to shoot and was a good friend.

There was a lady with the party, who was also a friend of the shoot owner and his family. As it was a nice day, she had come for a day out with us and brought her golden retriever to help a bit at the shoot. At the first drive she came and stood beside me chatting away while I shot at the pheasants coming over me, and her dog and mine picked up my shot birds afterwards. It was while we were walking to the last pheasant drive before lunch that this lady told me she had over-heard the other gun asking to borrow some cartridges. 'Take my advice, Hunter,' she said, 'and make sure you get your cartridges back from him, as he is not very good at returning things he borrows from other people.' I thanked her for her kind advice.

This lady loved working her golden retriever gun dog at a few different game shoots; she would normally stand beside a gun that didn't have a gun dog and her dog would pick up the shot game birds for them.

I used to meet this lady at different game shoots from time to time, and she and her dog were always in great demand, both because she was a very nice person and because good gun dogs are always very welcome at game shoots as they can always improve the enjoyment of the day. Some dog-handlers, if they themselves don't shoot and aren't taking their dog with the beating line, may be asked by the gamekeeper to pick up the shot birds from one of the guns that doesn't have a dog with them or they may be asked to try to find a wounded game bird that one of the guns thought, and said, they had shot. That was what this lady usually did. Picking up shot game birds for the guns at game shoots who don't have dogs with them can be a sort of privileged job at some game shoots.

Anyway, to revert to the Day of the Borrowed Cartridges, as lunchtime approached we all gathered together, guns, beaters, dog-handlers and the gamekeeper, to discuss the morning's sport and to count the bag. Then we walked over to the farm barn, where we sat at tables on long wooden benches to eat the lunch we had each brought with us and wash it down with the drinks provided by the shoot owner for anyone in need of refreshment. After an hour or so of eating and chatting we got up to go out again and resume shooting – but the guy who had borrowed the cartridges from me in the morning never offered me any back, as he had said he would.

Later on that afternoon the gamekeeper came to have a chat with me and asked if I was enjoying the shoot and getting plenty of shooting. I told him I was having an excellent day and was very much enjoying the good company – however, there was a rather delicate little matter that he might be able to help me with. When he asked what it was, I explained that one of the guests had borrowed thirty cartridges from me in the morning, saying he would give me them back at lunchtime, but that so far he hadn't done so. The gamekeeper said he already knew about this from the lady with the golden retriever.

'This is not the first time this person has borrowed cartridges from other guests and never returned them. Leave it to me, Hunter, and I will make sure you get your thirty cartridges. I will also tell my boss, the shoot owner, about it.'

After the shoot the guns and the guests were invited to a meal in the farmhouse before going home, and I was shedding my shooting gear at the car before going into the farmhouse when the keeper came and handed me back my thirty cartridges, saying that he hoped this matter hadn't spoiled my day's shooting. I replied that it certainly hadn't; I had thoroughly enjoyed my day, and my dog had worked well for me. I thanked him for the day, handed him a tip, £30, and went into the farmhouse to enjoy the meal and the company.

———•◆•———

At driven shoots one may come across a 'greedy' shot – and such people soon get a reputation! A greedy shot is someone who, when standing at a drive, not only shoots the birds that fly over them but also tries to shoot some of those flying over the guns who are standing on either side of them in the shooting line, who may be twenty-five metres or so away.

If you are unlucky enough to be on the receiving end of such arrogant and selfish behaviour, it can considerably diminish your enjoyment of a day's shooting.

At most driven shoots the guns stand beside a

numbered peg to shoot, and the number of the peg is decided by a draw that is conducted before the shoot starts. There are usually eight or nine numbered stands at each drive, and the same number of guns will have been invited to shoot. Before the proceedings start the host or the keeper goes round the guests shooting with eight or nine short sticks, rods or cards, each of which bears a number (which is initially concealed). Each guest is asked to pull a stick, and the number on the stick is the number of the peg at the first stand that he or she shoots from. After that they would normally go to a peg two numbers higher for the next drive (say, from 4 up to 6, or from 9 to 2). The purpose of the draw is to try to give each gun a good stand or two during the day (lots of birds may come over a particular number at one stand, and very few at another), or, if that doesn't work, to ensure that any inequity is caused only by the luck of the draw.

Normally, though, this system works quite well at most shoots and gives the guns a mixture of good and not-so-good stands.

The sets of short, numbered sticks used for the draw are an inch or two long and nowadays may be made of various materials, from metal to plastic. In the past some gamekeepers carved them from wood, bone, deer antlers or cattle horns. Some of the sets are beautifully carved and lovely to look at. They may be kept in a wooden box or a leather or canvas case, and on some shoots and estates these sets have been handed down over the generations.

If you happen to draw next to a greedy, selfish shooter, then you will be next to them all day, and they can affect your enjoyment of the day, especially if you are not as quick a shot as your greedy neighbour. At a partridge shoot a greedy shot can sometimes be partly avoided, because the keeper may ask guns to be ready to move a few metres to the left or right of their peg, depending on how the partridges fly that particular day, so you have to watch very carefully how the birds are flying and move if you think you need to. At a pheasant shoot, though, you stand at your peg until the end of the drive.

There are also shoots where they don't draw for peg numbers at the start of the day, but the landowner, the keeper or the shoot captain places the guns individually at each drive. This may be done to try to make sure that everyone gets a fair share of the shooting in the particular conditions of the day. However, it can sometimes turn out that if you look after the keeper, he will look after you; he will know how the birds fly, and so be able to see you are placed at some good stands where you will get plenty of shooting.

This is the way many small shoots and syndicates operate, and there will always be one or two guns nudging to get the stands where the best shooting is and never giving a thought to good manners or shooting etiquette. So, if you are a member of a syndicate or a paying guest at a pheasant shoot, just watch and look around to see what shooting you get on the first few drives compared to what shooting some of the other guns are getting. If you are not very happy about what you see going on and don't think you are getting a fair share of the shooting, then just don't go back to that shoot again. Alternatively, you may at a subsequent shoot have the opportunity tactfully to convey your thoughts about not enjoying yourself at the previous shoot to the gamekeeper or his assistant, and he or she will pass your comments on and this won't do you any harm.

If you are a paying member of a syndicate and you notice from time to time that one of the other members always seems to make for the stands where the most pheasants fly over, and you feel you are not getting a fair slice of the action, first of all let things be for a few shoots, just to see if it wasn't simply a one-off thing. If it does continue, though (and there are guns out there who do try to get the best positions for their own selfish advantage), then in most shooting syndicates you will probably find there is a head guy and a helper who places most of the guns on a shooting day. Have a quiet word with him about this chap hogging all the best stands.

Sometimes the head guy of the syndicate may not be able to do much about the situation for various reasons: for instance, the selfish gun may own the land; he may spend more time than other syndicate members feeding and looking after the pheasants; or he may have been part of the shoot long before any syndicate started. However, what he can do is try and make sure that the member who has complained to him is put at some good stands where he should get his share of the game shooting, and this should balance things out.

For many years I have been a guest at a pheasant shoot on the Scottish Border where the owners assign their guests to pegs before each drive. One of them will look around, call the name of the gun standing nearest to him, and ask that gun to stand, say, at the peg here or that one nearby. A regular member at this shoot has often suggested that one should stand back during this process, because he says, one gets a better stand by not pushing forward, for the last few names called normally get better stands and more shooting. I have never deliberately done that at this shoot, as jockeying to get a better stand to me is not etiquette and I wouldn't like my friends to even think I would do it. Having said that, though, I have had some good pheasant drives and some not-so-good drives at this shoot over the years, and I can't say that hanging back or not hanging back while the next drive was being sorted out has made any difference that I have noticed.

———•—•———

Over many years I have enjoyed the company of my friends and their families at many different shoots. In general it's a great sport, game shooting, and most of the people who take part in it are very nice and friendly.

The sport has evolved over the last fifty years or so, and its whole social structure has changed. Half a century ago the landowners and estate owners were the people that did most of the game shooting. They invited their friends and neighbours to their shoots, and everyone knew one another at the shoots and also socialized together at various other events. Then some farmers who owned their own farms took an interest in shooting and started rearing a few pheasants and inviting a few friends and neighbours for a shoot and a bit of tea afterwards. Soon after that a few more farmers began joining together, forming small syndicates to shoot the land collectively and rearing young pheasants at one of the farms. Then the farmers started to invite friends and business contacts to come and shoot with them, and they still do this today at small shoots and large.

Over the years, as interest in game shooting increased, and as the cost of rearing the game birds and managing them also increased, some estates and farmer shoots started letting out a day's pheasant shooting at so much a gun. This has now developed into big business, with people from Europe, America and from all over the United Kingdom paying a lot of money to go pheasant, grouse, partridge, and duck shooting. With some shoots now charging about £40 a head to shoot a pheasant and about £60 a head to shoot a grouse, letting shooting brings in much-needed money to estates and farms, and it seems that more and more people and companies are now wanting to take part in the sport of game shooting.

———•◆•———

The result of the process just described is that many people are now taking up shooting who are new to it. There's nothing wrong with that but one thing: the safety culture that should underlie shooting has not been ingrained in them through the process of learning it in youth. So, it is vital that the safety and etiquette of this country sport is maintained and upheld in these new circumstances. (The etiquette is important too, because it is essentially founded on safety, plus that element of 'do-as-you-would-be-done-by' that is important in every area of life.)

One of the greatest dangers in shooting is that of injuring other people. These might be other guns on either side, beaters in front, pickers-up out behind, or people who just happen to be walking along a nearby public footpath – and not all of them will necessarily even be visible (they might be masked from view by a fence or a bush or a tree). This is why it is dangerous when people shoot at game birds that are flying too low, swinging their gun round following the birds until at the moment when they pull the trigger the muzzle may be pointing at another human being – perhaps their neighbour in the shooting line. This does happen at pheasant, partridge and grouse shoots and is extremely dangerous.

At some pheasant shoots I go to, the guns are

instructed not to shoot any ground game, such as hares and rabbits, just for safety and because of the number of gun dogs at the shoot, and before most shoots start the keeper, the landowner or the person in charge will give a short safety briefing and tell the guns not to shoot any low birds.

Shooting at low birds is very dangerous, but it does happen all too often. Holding my hand on my heart I can't honestly say that I have never, ever shot at a low pheasant, and I'm sure most regular game shooters will say the same. What one should do, though, is to be constantly vigilant and aware of the danger.

What I always do at shoots is think safety. When I go to a stand to shoot pheasants, partridges or grouse I first look forward, to see where the birds will be coming from; I look behind and around me, to see where the nearest guns and pickers-up are standing; and I am also very much aware of where the beaters will be coming from. I also take notice of the ground. If it's not level, will I be able to shoot without slipping and causing an accident? This safety checking seems to have served me well over the years.

I can remember a pheasant shoot a few years ago when it was very wet and windy, and the ground was very slippery. Another gun and myself were standing on a bank shooting at the pheasants that were being flushed over us. I happened to look across at the other gun and saw him trying to pick himself up from the ground; he had slipped and fallen over as he was shooting at some pheasants flying over him.

I called over to ask if he was alright, and he said he was, but he was going home to change his Wellington boots, because the soles of the ones he had on were so worn that they had no tread or grip left, which was why he had slipped and fallen. He said it was too dangerous to carry on in those boots. (Luckily, he owned a farm next-door to the shoot, so he hadn't far to go to change them.) I was very impressed with this farmer. How right he was to see the safety of people as more important than the pheasant shooting!

At many pheasant shoots early in the season the birds sometimes don't lift and fly very high, and this is where the guns have to be very selective in not shooting – although all through the season they should think safety and be careful about which pheasants they choose to shoot at. For example, once dogs have flushed the pheasants a few times, the cock pheasants in particular get to know what's going on when the beaters appear, and they may take evasive measures, like running along the ground and doubling back, or flying out of the side of the wood about dog height; it is particularly dangerous to shoot at these low birds.

Another danger can arise if a bird is flying across in front of a wood or a thick covert, dropping as it flies. If the gun can't see what's in or beyond the thick cover, then it's not safe to shoot.

I keep harping on about gun safety and will continue to do so. Young people are coming into the sport and so are newcomers from all walks of life, and one gun accident in the field is far too many. With the influx of new people taking up shooting in the countryside, the safety culture and the etiquette of the sport are sometimes not as sound or solid as they were when my father was shooting and taught them to me while I was being brought up in the countryside.

7

Shooting Clothes
and Cartridges

There is a great variety of shooting clothes to cope with all types of weather and conditions that one might meet out shooting. Even so, when one is out in strong wind and heavy rain it can be most unpleasant. With the rain blowing into my face and water starting to drip down the back of my neck, I have often wondered, 'What the hell am I doing here?'

Some shooting accessories are not easy to get hold of these days. I can remember many years ago my father wearing gaiters when he went shooting, especially grouse shooting. These fitted round the calf of each leg, fastening down one side with leather straps, from below the knee to the top of the boot or shoe. They were made of stout leather (finer ones were made of horse skin) and were worn over trousers or with breeches and knee-length woollen stockings to keep the legs dry when walking in long, wet vegetation and to protect them from the scratches and pricks of brambles, gorse, heather, bracken or rushes.

Many farmers and farm workers (ploughmen, too) used to wear gaiters, and some polished them with brown boot polish until they shone like new pennies. Others had gaiters that never saw a lick of polish and were tied up with bits of string or binder twine but still protected their legs and kept them clean and dry in all weather.

Gaiters went out of fashion around the 1950s and 1960s and just seemed to disappear. From time to time I used to see the odd pair of gaiters in an antique shop in quite good condition, and then in 2006 at the Royal Highland Show at Edinburgh I spotted the stand of a French store that had all sorts of leather sporting goods – cartridge bags and belts, dog leads, leather coats and jackets, leather-clad shooting sticks – and there they were, leather gaiters at £60 a pair. It was great to see them.

Brown leather gaiters may be hard to find these days, but good-quality waterproof canvas ones are easily available and are ideal for wearing with boots or stout shoes in all weathers for shooting, fishing, walking and all country sports. They are tough, lightweight, water-resistant and very comfortable to wear.

Footwear is very important for safety when you are out shooting, and should always have good grips or tread on the soles. Weather conditions and the time of year will often determine the type of footwear you should wear for the type of game shooting you are going to do.

The grouse season starts on 12 August, and the weather at that time of year is often very mild, and if you are standing in butts shooting driven grouse, then a pair of good strong shoes with sturdy soles can be ideal, though for walked-up grouse shooting over dogs I normally wear boots.

I can remember at one time you could buy a good heavy type of brown shoe with a tongue flap that covered the laces and stopped any bits of debris working into the shoe. Many gamekeepers used to wear this type of shoe with long stockings year round in all weathers, but I haven't seen it for a long time now.

The brogue is a heavy-soled leather outdoor shoe with decorative patterns of holes punched in the outer layer of leather. Many gamekeepers and country folk wore brogues all the time, for they are strong, sturdy and comfortable to wear, and they look good and help to protect your ankles.

Boots seem to be the most common shooting footwear today, and there is a great variety on the market to choose from. Shop around, but buy a waterproof pair and go for ones you like and feel comfortable wearing, for shooting boots can have a hard life in the field.

I use good-quality, sturdy brown boots, and I always buy my shooting footwear one size bigger than indoor shoes, to allow for the thick knee-length stockings I wear for shooting.

I remember there used to be a heavy working boot with turned-up toes ('sprung'), steel toe-caps and sturdy soles in which there were rows and rows of hobnails or tackets. These were worn by shepherds, farmers and some gamekeepers, and they were good for all weathers. We used to say you could climb up the side of a house in these boots without hanging on, as the toes were so well turned up.

There is also a great variety of Wellington boots on the market for country buffs of all ages, with prices varying for different designs and colours. I normally wear green or blue Wellington boots on the farm and at some shoots with a pair of waterproof overtrousers as well if I know it is going to be wet; the overtrousers keep my legs dry above the knee, and at lunch time, or at the end of a shooting day, it is quite easy to pull the waterproof trousers down over the Wellington tops and take the boots off, leaving everything just ready to step back into when needed.

Some game shooters wear a pair of wax waterproof leggings that fasten down one side, each legging suspended by a strap that goes over your trouser belt and fastens with a stud.

Shooting jackets come in many varieties. Some have an outer layer of tweed or artificial fibre and a waterproof layer of Gore-Tex underneath, others are made of waxed cotton. The latter are still very popular indeed with game shooters. The ladies and men who fish also wear them as do many farmers, hikers and members of the horsy brigade, not to mention the general public.

I wear both waxed and tweed jackets. I wear the waxed jacket with overtrousers for working on the farm, and from time to time when they get mucky I hose the dirty parts down using a scrubbing brush. When I go shooting I wear a tweed jacket no matter what the weather conditions are like, as I find it warm and comfortable. (I do have a light waterproof jacket with me, but I don't often use it.) When it is really wet it gets very heavy and can sometimes take about a week to dry out in the shed or in the cow byre. (You shouldn't dry these types of clothes beside a fire: let them dry out naturally.)

I normally wear a variety of baseball caps with

my shooting clothes (normally pull-on waterproofs) and can face any type of weather with them.

————•◆•————

I am often asked what type of cartridges I use. As far as the size of shot is concerned, this depends a great deal on what particular game birds or ground game I am going after.

More generally, though, cartridges have changed a great deal for the better over the last sixty years or so. Apart from their metal bases, cartridge cases used to be made of stout paper, and if they got damp or wet they used to swell. This led to the loss of time at crucial moments when reloading the gun because it was difficult or impossible to get the swollen cartridge into the chamber of the barrel – and then they might stick in the chamber after firing, which could strain the shotgun's ejector mechanism. Many a time I've then had the job of trying to get empty cartridge cases out of the gun by using a screw-driver, pliers or sometimes a long bit of strong plain fencing wire that I threaded down from the opposite end of the gun barrel to try and push the empty cartridge case out of the breech. Today's cartridges have plastic cases, which don't swell when they get damp, and so are much quicker to handle and shoot with.

The shot size I use in my cartridges depends, as I say, on what game I am trying to shoot, the direction in which it is likely to be moving, and of course the range. Birds flying towards me are easier to kill (provided I am pointing the gun straight) because the range is decreasing when the shot is fired and because a bird's head and neck are thinly covered with feathers, so that just a few shotgun pellets will kill it. But if a bird is flying across in front of me the range is not closing and also it may take more shotgun pellets to bring it down because the feathers are thicker on the body than the head. Much the same is true of birds flying away from me, only the range is increasing when the shot is fired. I use 12-bore shotguns which are now very common.

When I am shooting wild ducks I use No. 4 shot, either steel or bismuth (it is now against the law to shoot wildfowl with lead shot, even if you own your own lake, pond, river or marshland). Steel shot cartridges can be three or four times the price of lead shot cartridges and there are various opinions as to how good they are (some people think steel shot is not as good as the lead shot used to be and doesn't bring the ducks down as well), but the law is the law!

I buy the steel No. 4 or bismuth shot

cartridges for my guests when I invite them to come and shoot ducks at my ponds.

Wild mallard in full plumage are quite a living feather bed and can take some stopping, which is why I use a larger shot size for them than for other species. Wild ducks approaching can be easier to shoot, because the head and face are less protected, but crossing ducks can be more difficult because of the tightly packed feathers on the body, and should not be shot at too great a range. Duck that are going away are harder still, and quite a concentration of shotgun pellets is needed to stop them.

Nonetheless, my experience is that No. 4 steel or bismuth shot fired from a 12-bore shotgun will bring ducks down if the aim is accurate and the range not too great.

When shooting pheasants I use the slightly smaller No. 6 lead shot. I find this weight of shot can stop most flying pheasant and doesn't damage the birds. On a stormy, windy day the best of game shots can find that high pheasants, flying overhead or crossing, can take some stopping. The wind can make them fly like rockets and twist and swerve as well, but No. 6 shot will bring them down if the aim is true.

In fact No. 6 is a good shot size for most game shooting in most conditions. Shop around for your cartridges, though, as they vary a great deal in price. Also, buying a larger quantity, say two hundred and fifty or five hundred, will be cheaper per cartridge than a box of twenty-five.

Partridges are a smaller bird than pheasants, but I use No. 6 shot for them as well, although some people like a smaller shot size. I find No. 6 does perfectly well and doesn't damage the shot birds. The secret of shooting driven partridges is to try and get as close to the approaching birds as possible by being in the right place. You may be allowed to move a few metres sideways from your numbered peg, and you should keep quiet and out of sight, because a covey of partridges may split or veer off if the birds see you as they approach.

When I go grouse shooting, either walked-up over dogs or driven grouse, I again use No. 6 shot. Grouse in their winter dress, in November towards the end of the season, are very well feathered and insulated against the winter arctic elements. Driven grouse, approaching the guns very fast and low, can swing and dip, dive and change direction in a moment, so they can take some hitting, but well-aimed No. 6 shot will do it. And if packs of grouse are flushed some distance out from the guns, by the time they reach the butts they can reach full speed and be over the butts in seconds and test the best of shots, because you don't have much time to shoot at them.

Grouse walked-up and shot over dogs can look like fast-moving black balls of feathers, and they have to be hit with a concentration of pellets to bring them down, and birds that are going away are more difficult as the range increases. Crossing birds, flying fairly high with the wind at their tails, can take a good shot to bring them down, too, for they will be twisting and swaying in the wind.

My experience at shooting grouse has been fairly successful over the years, shooting with a 12-bore side-by-side shotgun and No. 6 shot. But there are still the birds I miss (and that's quite a lot), but it's not the fault of the cartridges. You need a lot of concentration with grouse.

Snipe, too, are rather special, and I enjoy snipe shooting very much. For these smaller birds I normally use the smaller No. 7 shot, which, if I can hit the snipe, will bring the bird down without doing too much damage.

I used to shoot snipe quite a lot in Scotland. We had this large 100-acre (40-hectare) marsh and swamp next door to the farm, which was a very popular place for snipe and many other types of wildlife. My dogs used to enjoy nothing better than working in the marsh, quartering the ground and flushing snipe in all weathers; even when the ground was covered with ice during a hard frost there was always the odd snipe lying for the dogs to flush.

The cattle, too, enjoyed grazing the marsh. In a dry summer I have seen them standing in the marsh up to their bellies in mud. At one time there was talk of draining parts of the marsh for agricultural use, but this was soon dismissed when it was noticed how well the cattle did on the marsh, and so it was left wild, a sanctuary for the sportsman and for this small bird with its curious call and baffling flight, so different from that of any other bird.

I have shot snipe over dogs and had the birds flushed over me many times, and there is a great knack in picking the best time to fire at a lifting or flushed snipe. When the bird lifts it usually shows the white of its underneath plumage for a second, just before it gets the full air speed it needs to take evasive action.

This is the moment to shoot before the snipe starts its fork lightning display of erratic, side-to-side jinking, and then, well out of gunshot, suddenly rises high in the sky and is safe.

Turning to ground game, I normally use No. 6 shot for both hares and rabbits. I have walked up hares and shot them over my gun dogs for many years and been to many driven hare shoots too. My father used to tell me not to shoot hares up the backside when they were going away from me, as I would only wound them. He told me when aiming the gun to swing the gun barrel through the hare and past the tip of its ears, and then fire – advice I have found very helpful over the years.

This question comes up so often in the field of how much lead, or follow-through, to give a crossing hare or rabbit, or how much lead to give game birds that are crossing or being flushed overhead. This is a question of experience. I can't say that you should give a hare or game bird so many metres lead, swinging your gun through it then keeping going before you fire. The answer will vary with the circumstances of each shot – height, speed, distance and umpteen other things – but the rule of thumb is, if you are not hitting a crossing hare or game bird, then you are not giving it enough lead. Lots of game is missed because the shooter pokes at the target with his shotgun and doesn't follow through. I do it myself from time to time, so I know! So success comes down to experience: the more game you shoot, the better you will become.

Hares have a very keen sense of smell and

good hearing. On a hare drive I have seen the hares moving towards the guns, then, when still out of gunshot, sniffing the air and breaking back through the beaters to safety. Brown hares are animals of habit, and like old meadow fields with rough grass and rushes. They often lie beside a hedge or fence so that they can escape easily and leave the dogs puzzling over where they have gone. They sleep in among rough grasses or some rushes in ploughed fields or just inside the edge of a wood where they can escape easily. A hare makes a nest or bed by flattening the grass or vegetation in an impression, known as its 'form', which is just an imprint of its shape.

Hares are very well camouflaged. I have often come across one away out in the middle of a ploughed field with no cover around it, but, because of its brown colour, I couldn't see it until either it lifted or (if I was walking into the wind) I was on top of it.

8

Gamekeepers and Vermin

A gamekeeper has to have skills that go beyond rearing and looking after game birds. The farmers, shepherds, farm workers and villagers are all well worth getting along with, if he wants to be successful. Goodwill is something we should all carry in our pockets every day, and lots of it. This was drummed into me when I was a boy by my father, who always told me to be nice to people and treat them as I wanted to be treated myself.

There are nowhere near as many people working in the countryside now as there were some forty years ago. Over that period thousands have left the land to try and better themselves with jobs in the towns and cities. But I don't think the countryside is a better place for the loss of all these families from the countryside, for we have lost a lot of good workers and their valuable skills. Builders of stone walls, masons, plumbers, electricians, drainers, fencers, tractor drivers, painters and breeders of quality live-stock are only a few of the skills that were lost, along with some real worthy country characters who exercised them. The countryside has become more mechanized and now needs a lot fewer farm workers, but those that are left, still working on the land, are much more highly skilled in many different ways than those who migrated to the town many years ago.

A number of farm workers still help game-keepers on the shooting days by beating (or working their gun dogs) to earn some extra money, although farm workers today are far better paid than some of them forty years ago; in those days some farm workers would now and again try and trap a rabbit or a pheasant for the pot, just to get a taste of meat for the family, without the game-keeper's knowing anything about it.

I have known some gamekeepers who were very badly liked and caused all sorts of problems on the estates they worked for, because the tenant farmers and the estate and farm workers hated them. One, who worked on a small estate on the Scottish border, was suspicious of every-body who went near the estate; he didn't even trust his own mother when she came to stay with him for a few days. There were five farm tenants on the estate, six farm workers, a couple of estate workers and a shepherd, and this gamekeeper caused no end of trouble with one of the tenant farmers, who had the right to graze his sheep on the moor, and his shepherd. The shepherd had worked for the tenant farmer for nearly thirty years, long before this pompous ass of a game-keeper came to the estate. The farm in question was right on the fringe of the moor, and the 200-odd sheep were kept on the grouse moor most of the year. The shepherd only brought them back down to the farm for shearing, or if it was a very hard winter, when he would feed them around the farm buildings until the weather improved.

The keeper was always complaining to the shepherd, about his bloody dogs and sheep on the moor. The shepherd was a nice guy and could tolerate quite a lot, but this keeper was just not a nice person, so he found a way of getting his own back: he used to round his sheep up on the moor in the spring, when the moor should be left quiet because the grouse and the other birds are sitting on eggs. Many nests and eggs were smashed by the sheep and the shepherd's two collie dogs.

The keeper sometimes complained to the tenant farmer about his shepherd trampling all over the moor with his dogs scaring the grouse off the moor, but the farmer more or less told the keeper to buzz off and left it like that. So one day the keeper and the shepherd had a punch up, and the shepherd felled the gamekeeper. This was just a few days before the landowner had arranged to have one of only about three grouse shoots he held each year. My father was invited to this shoot, and I was going along to work my dogs, and when we arrived on the day, we could see the keeper had a beauty of a black eye and a badly cut lip.

Good relations with farmers, farm workers and neighbours are also very important for the game-keepers on lower ground, where pheasant and partridge shooting goes on. They are likely to have more contact with people than moorland keepers.

It is most important that a lower ground gamekeeper has good relations with those he is in contact with as it can be quite easy for a poacher to be tipped off where pheasant and partridge are being reared.

I recall one really good low-ground keeper: a nice guy, who tried to get on with everyone around him and was very well liked. He worked on a small country estate of a few thousand acres, consisting of three tenanted farms and the home farm, which was run by a farm manager. There were two woodmen on the estate and a few farm workers on the farms and the home farm. Every year the keeper raised 500 pheasants from day-old chicks.

It was a family estate, and the shooting guests were normally friends and a few business acquaintants. I first met this gamekeeper at another pheasant shoot, where he was beating and helping out a keeper friend and colleague, and I was shooting and working my dogs.

There were two shot pheasants that couldn't be found, and I was asked if I could help find them. I had my springer spaniel Patch with me that day, and he was a really good gun dog: if dead pheasants were around, he would find them. The keeper from the shoot told me where he was pretty sure the birds had dropped, and I set Patch on to find them.

I first checked the wind direction and took Patch thirty metres or so downwind of where the pheasant had dropped, turned him and started working him upwind to try and pick up the bird's scent. As we got near where it was thought to have dropped, Patch showed interest, and I knew the pheasant was somewhere about by his body movements and his slightly wagging tail. He pushed on for another twenty metres or so towards a small patch of scrub. He was into this like a shot and after a few moments came out looking at me and wagging his tail; I told the keeper the pheasant was in the scrub and was probably stuck in a tree somewhere. Sure enough, it had dropped into this thick scrub and lodged in a fork about two metres above the ground, which was why the other dogs hadn't been able to find it.

Finding the first pheasant hadn't taken all that long, but the second one wasn't so easy. Again I checked the wind and went some forty metres or so downwind of where the bird had dropped, then turned the dog and started working him into the wind to try and pick up the scent. He showed some interest as we got near the point of fall, wagging his tail at me once or twice and pushing on a bit faster; this told me the pheasant had hit the ground but then picked itself up and started running. I encouraged Patch to follow the line of scent, and he ran on for about forty metres or so, and then suddenly stopped at a scrubby patch of nettles, rushes and docks and wagged his tail and looked at me. I knew from this that the pheasant was there somewhere, so I went and had a look among the rushes and docks and saw two rabbit burrows. I said to Patch, 'where is the pheasant then?' and he pushed his nose down one of the burrows and wagged his tail.

I pushed my hand and arm into the burrow and felt the shot pheasant, which was still alive. I pulled it out and handed it to the keeper, who pulled its neck and killed it.

I never thought any more about the two finds, and Patch and I went on to have a very good day. He made some very good retrieves and found a few lost game birds; to me this was what game shooting is all about. But what I didn't know was that the keeper from the private estate had been watching the two of us at work most of the day. He made a point of having a few words with me now and again during the day, but I didn't think anything of it, as lots of people come and talk to me at most game shoots.

When shooting was over for the day and we were in the farmhouse having tea before going home, this keeper from the private estate came over to me again and asked if I would like to come and help him at his pheasant shoots with my dog. They only had three or four pheasant shoots a year, he said, and his boss would be very pleased for me to shoot at one of them and help him beating and picking up at the others. (Picking up involves being asked to stand beside guns who have no gun dog with them to retrieve their shot birds, or else to wait back behind the shooting line to find lost game birds at the end of a grouse or pheasant drive.) For me this was the start of a long and friendly relationship with this keeper and the estate owners.

Sometimes when he was rearing the young pheasants he would ring up and ask if I would come and give him a hand moving the pheasant chicks into new pens. I was always pleased to go and help, whether the job was moving pheasant chicks, washing and repairing pheasant rearing pens, catching vermin, or going picking up or beating with my gun dog on shooting days.

I used to take a dog with me whenever I went to help him on the estate. It was an excellent education for a young gun dog being among the pheasant chicks and a great opportunity for it to acquire the discipline it would need in its working career. Sometimes I used to tether the dog to the wire inside the pheasant pen and drive some of the young pheasants past it very slowly while instructing it to sit and not to touch. Or sometimes, before the pheasants could fly, I used to put the dog on a long rope, and we would round the pheasants up very slowly in the pheasant pen, just like rounding up ducks, geese or sheep. That was wonderful training and experience for any gun dog.

———•———

If some of a keeper's duties involve arranging shooting days and rearing pheasants, others are concerned with maintaining or improving the habitat of his game: heather-burning for grouse, as we have seen, or draining, or maintaining woodland. He also needs to protect his game against predators – some of whom can be human. Poaching in the countryside, either for the pot or to sell the game, has been going on for as long as the concept of 'game' (meaning all birds and beasts that are both used as food for man and are usually shot or hunted by man for sport). In the past the pot poachers, who took a rabbit, hare, pheasant or salmon for food, were often farm and estate workers or sometimes villagers who knew something about the coun- tryside and sometimes helped on the farms during hay and harvest time – so they got to know if pheasants were being reared on the estate or near the farm where they were working. Some of these poachers led the landowners and keepers a merry dance from time to time, as they were very crafty and skilled, and they knew the lie of the land they were poaching on. I used to know a couple of well-known so-called poachers, and they were very well liked in the neighbourhood. They liked their ale, and I never knew either of them do any work; they lived on their wits and from their friends.

Perhaps more common nowadays are the people who combine poaching with stealing anything they can from the countryside for money (from stone slates off barn roofs to diesel fuel). Those are just villains and normally come from the towns and cities. The money poachers may drive out into the countryside to see what is going on, and if they see lots of pheasants running about in the fields they mark the spot and come back another night at dusk with a van.

Pheasants don't normally roost too high up in the trees, and many of them may still be in the rearing pens sitting on top of low branches and on top of the feeders or on bales of straw. The poachers can easily catch a few pheasants and wring their necks quietly and be in and out of the wood or covert with a sack or two full of pheasants in a very short time, and they will have a ready market for their pheasants.

These people who poach and steal from the farms and the countryside don't care what damage they do as long as they can steal something to sell. Farmers have to lock up all their sheds and outhouses or lose almost any sort of equipment: quad bikes, batteries, trailers and many different types of tools – anything worth any money will be stolen if not locked up.

———•·———

Most of the non-human predators on game come under the heading of vermin. If you want to keep a good stock of game on your shoot, then you have to control the vermin. As soon as game begins to increase on your shoot, vermin of all sorts will arrive upon the scene – where it comes from is one of the countryside's mysteries, but come it will.

The stoat is a very efficient killer. It's not often that one sees it at work, but it will kill game chicks, rabbits, mice and other ground nesting birds. Stoats are about 44 cm long, from the head to the tip of their tail and in the north they partly change colour from red-brown to white in the winter – except for the tip of the tail, which is a tuft of long black hairs all the year round.

It has been thought for some time that the stoat's change of colour depends a great deal on the temperature. In some parts of Scotland where there are regular falls of snow the animal goes completely white, except for the black tail tip. But I have noticed over the past thirty odd years in the north that, where we don't get regular falls of snow, some stoats I have seen are only partly white in winter. But if the temperature does affect the change in the stoat's colour, it must be the temperature of the *previous* winter and the length of the day, as the new white coat grows underneath the old one before the animal moults in the autumn.

The stoat hunts across moors and heaths along hedgerows, across fields and riverbanks, among farm buildings and along stone walls, wherever there is a chance they may catch some food. I have seen what killers these explosive little animals can be, and what determined characters they are. We had a small rowan tree in the farm orchard in which a woodpigeon had built a nest about three metres from the ground. When I found the nest there were two newly hatched pigeon chicks in it, and I cut back a few tree branches in front of it, so that I could sit at the cow byre window a few metres away and watch the young chicks being fed.

It was a very dry summer that year, and it was great fun watching the young pigeon chicks growing up. Then, one evening while I was sitting watching the nest near dusk, I happened to see this stoat coming towards me in the orchard. Before I knew what was happening it was up the tree, killed both chicks in the nest, then tossed one of them out, climbed down the tree and ate most of the young pigeon before bouncing off like a shot.

Stoats hunt by scent and they also have good hearing, but not very good eyesight. They can travel for miles, and gamekeepers need to be on their guard against this tyrant of the country-side, for it will kill anything it finds in its path.

The weasel is another explosive little predator, smaller than its cousin the stoat and without the black tip on its tail. The upper parts of its body are a reddish brown and it has a white belly. It doesn't roam as far over the countryside and likes hunting among old farm buildings, along hedgerows and along stone walls. The male weasel weighs about 115 gm.

The weasel eats a great variety of prey, such as mice, rats, moles, frogs, small birds' eggs, poultry chicks and game chicks if they can get in among them. However, I don't think weasels do as much damage among the game birds as stoats. I have caught more stoats than weasels around my pheasant pens.

The weasel is fairly easy to trap and control, because it is a very inquisitive little animal. If it is disturbed it will quickly dash for cover, but then, if you stand still and wait a few moments, it will reappear to see what scared it in the first place; this is when the weasel can be shot, and some are shot if they are causing trouble.

I once saw a weasel kill a rat that was crossing

the farmyard. The weasel seemed to come from nowhere, jumped onto the rat's back and sank its teeth into the back of its head; after they had both rolled over once or twice the rat was dead. The rat was about three times the size of the weasel.

The dogs used to chase the weasels on the farm, but I have never known them catch one, because the weasels are so quick, and they can escape into a very small hole or gap. There are fewer weasels on farms today, because there are fewer rats and mice on the farms, so the weasels have spread further into the countryside and hunt more along hedgerows, riverbanks, barns, stone walls and old buildings.

Another undesirable, from the keeper's point of view, is the rat. Rats are very dirty creatures and are much associated with quarries, sewers, rubbish tips, docks and farms. There are two types of rat in this country. The first, the black rat (also known as the ship rat), probably originates from India, it weighs about 200 gm and is often found around docks. The second, and more common, is the larger brown rat, or common rat, which, despite its Latin misnomer of *rattus norvegicus*, originally came not from Scandinavia but from central Asia.

Around the 1960s and 1970s there were

always rats on farms, and plenty of them, but as agriculture changed, the grain on many farms was stored in large metal containers or silos, instead of barns and straw stacks, and the rats lost access to their regular good supply. As a result they spread out more into the countryside, being an adaptable species. They still breed on some farms but you will now find brown rats breeding in woods, along riverbanks, wherever young pheasants are being reared and fed on grain, and along the fringes of the moors and hills. They are now a problem on some grouse moors, when they eat the eggs of the red and the black grouse; a number of moor and hill keepers have been reporting seeing rats in increasing numbers on the hills and moors.

The fox is a cunning animal and pretty good at looking after itself, which makes it a particular problem for the keepers. From head to tail the fox is about 100 cm long and weighs about 6 kg. It is a night hunter and nowadays can be found in most towns and cities as well as in the countryside. It eats a great range of food, but in the country its main food is rabbits, frogs, beetles, game birds and chicks, lambs, farmyard ducks, hens and geese, and any eggs it finds and a variety of other things including worms, rodents and fruit. In the towns it eats lots of food scraps left around by humans (some people even put food out for the foxes in their gardens).

Being a night hunter in the countryside the fox will lie up during the day in a rabbit burrow or a badger sett or maybe among some rocks, while city foxes lie up under garden sheds, bridges, dwellings and flats. Anywhere they find a hole they will make a home; they are not all that particular where they live as long as they think they won't get disturbed.

The male, or dog, fox is slightly larger than the female (vixen). During winter nights one may hear the dog fox – he utters a sort of sharp bark that you can quite easily miss, but the loud, eerie scream of the vixen on a dark calm night will make your hair stand on end.

Moor and hill keepers are always on the lookout for trouble with foxes, but the fox often causes more trouble for the upland farmers and shepherds by killing new-born lambs in the spring. It is probably the low-ground keepers who suffer more, as foxes will kill game chicks or game birds in quantity if they get in among them in a rearing ground or in a release pen. The fox doesn't kill just what it intends to eat immediately; it will kill every bird or animal around if it moves – it is a killing machine. I have known a fox get into one of our hen houses, with some thirty-odd hens in it, and kill them all in a very short time.

We had the hen houses in a field some two or three hundred metres from the farm buildings, and the hens were shut in every night and let out first thing the next morning. We didn't very often have trouble with foxes, but when they did get in they slaughtered everything they could catch.

Since fox hunting was banned in February 2005, many foxes are now shot in the countryside at dusk or later with a rifle and a powerful torch. This is known as lamping. The gamekeeper, farmer or shepherd will go out in the dark, when foxes are hunting on the moors or on the farms. They try to catch a fox in the torch beam, which reflects back from its eyes as the fox freezes in the light, and then kill it with a shot from the rifle.

The badger is an animal that has become better known whether for good or the bad. It gets the blame for spreading brucellosis among cattle, and there has been much debate on the matter, and I am sure there will be much more in the future.

I have a badger that comes into my duck pond every night for a feed of wheat or barley. I also have a badger that tries to get into my pheasant pen by digging underneath the wire each night. I am not sure if the second one is trying to get into the pen to feed on the pheasant food or to kill the young pheasants, so I don't take any chances and keep the pen wire well pegged down.

Badgers are omnivorous. They will eat roots, beetles, grubs, slugs, fruitworms, rats, young rabbits, eggs and young game birds: they eat more or less anything they can catch. They weigh about 11 kg, and the female badger is called a sow and the male a boar. I have never heard any gamekeeper complaining about having lots of game bird chicks being killed by badgers, so they are more of a nuisance than anything else. Badger hair was once used for making paint-brushes and shaving brushes, and the skin of the badger was used for various purposes, including making pistol cases and sporrans.

I see badgers on a regular basis and I have weighed many dead badgers. For me, they bring a certain charm to the countryside, and they are lovely animals to watch at dusk.

9

The Hills and Moors

Driving over the moors, one's first reaction might be, 'What a barren, lovely-looking wilderness, but how can anything possibly live here except sheep or cattle?' Perhaps you have to be a gamekeeper, shepherd or farmer, someone who really knows about the moors, to see their full beauty and complexity, but at certain times of year they can be as busy as a city centre. The coming and going of some birds every year between the lowlands or the coast and their breeding grounds in the hills, and the coming and going of the resident birds and animals make the moors a fascinating place to watch and study a great variety of wildlife and different habitats. I have been surrounded by hills and moors all my life and have spent a lot of my time among their birds and animals.

Over the last thirty years or so the winters have become much milder on the moors. Before that there were some winters when the moors would be covered with heavy falls of snow early in the winter or early in the spring, accompanied by very hard frost. I once saw some red grouse sitting nearly on our doorstep looking for food, because conditions on the hills and moors were so terrible. But, if they can look very bleak in winter, in the summer, when the heather is in full bloom, its rich red/purple/pink tones give them a charming warm colour and the enticing aroma of heather honey.

One of the wild birds to be seen on the hills and moors is the black grouse, a substantial bird, about twice the size of red grouse, that lives on the upland fringe between hill farmland, moor and woodland. But these birds have been in decline for the last fifty years and more, due to the decline of mixed farming and the rise of forestry, among other reasons. They like open sweeps of land and moors, and some of those sweeps of land have been broken up by tree plantations, many of them consisting not of native deciduous trees but of fir trees, which make dark, cold woods that no game birds are happy in. Black grouse like smaller, open woods where they can roost and play around and feed on the insects.

Over the past fifty years or so many of these conifer woods have been planted on the hills and moors with the help of government planting grants and estate duty concessions, introduced to increase home-grown timber production. A good deal of the softwood used to be cut to make pit props for the coal mines.

Many of them were also planted to act as shelter belts for cattle and sheep (they also provided shelter for some wildlife species, such as foxes and squirrels), and in this role they were a great help to landowners and farmers during those very hard winters of the past. (It may be hard to believe, but in one winter in the 1970s the sheep that had been standing in deep snow were found dead and frozen solid. It was pitiful, too, to see thousands of dead birds on the moors that winter that had died of starvation.)

The conifer plantations did save a lot of wild life and sheep, but as they grew up they slowly helped to change the habitat of the black grouse, so the birds started to leave.

Overgrazing of heather moorland through the years by red deer and, particularly, sheep has also been thought to be partly to blame for the reduction of the black (and red) grouse, as these animals crop the vegetation so close to the ground that they affect its growth and reduce the caterpillars and other insects that the young grouse chicks need and feed on.

Another factor has been the decline of mixed farming and arable farming in the uplands. Black grouse sought out fields of oats, potatoes and turnips growing along the fringe of the moors, as they liked to eat the leaves of the turnips, to scratch among the potatoes for insects and to go onto the stooks and stubbles in the winter months to feed on the dislodged grains of corn still lying on the ground. Indeed, in a very hard winter the corn stubbles were the saving of much moorland wildlife, because they were never ploughed out until the following spring, and so provided wild birds and animals with a sure source of food on the fringe of the moors.

But, as agriculture changed, many hill farmers on the moorland fringes stopped growing turnips, corn and potatoes, because they involved a lot of hard manual work, and lots of the agricultural workers were leaving the land to seek a better life in the towns and cities. Both red and black grouse had been used to feeding on the farmland on the fringe of the moors but now the red grouse proved better able to cope with the agricultural changes than the black grouse. Both birds eat heather and bilberry shoots and the berries of such moorland plants as crowberry and bilberry, along with various insects. But in the spring black grouse also like the white seed heads of the cotton grass, which grows on the fringe of some heather moors, and later on the seeds of rushes and long grasses. They will also take to the trees to eat hazel catkins and the buds of larch and birch trees but the food they got from the farm land was a good part of their staple diet and when this became less plentiful some black grouse moved on.

Another reason for the decline of black grouse, and something that also kills a lot of the red grouse, is the wire netting that farmers and shepherds rig up along the tops of stone walls to stop the sheep scrambling over (and damaging the walls as they do so). Black and red grouse can fly straight into this wire netting and kill themselves, especially when it's misty and foggy and the birds are flying low and fast. This can be avoided by tying strips of metal reflectors onto the wire as this makes it more visible to the approaching birds.

Black grouse are very conservative in their habitats and generally select a particular spot for their fighting matches and frolicking around in the spring of the year. On these display grounds (referred to as leks) the black-and-white cock birds (blackcock) stake out small patches of ground where they call and display to attract females in for mating, fanning out their lyre-shaped tails. The females (greyhens) are a mottled brown in colour, and they nest in thick ground cover normally not more than a mile or so from the lek. The average brood size is between one and two chicks, which hatch in June and initially feed on insects and seeds. They remain in the family group or covey for about three months or so before becoming independent, and they live for about four to five years if they are not shot before that.

There are now a number of black grouse recovery projects going on in the north of England, Scotland and Wales to try and get more black grouse breeding on the hills and moors. Project officers in these areas can advise landowners and managers how they can help to bring more black grouse to the uplands, and they normally get good co-operation, for most hill and moor owners would like to see more black grouse on their ground. Measures that can be taken to help their recovery include planting hardwoods such as oak and beech on the fringes of conifer plantations and creating open spaces within them for black grouse and other wildlife.

————•————

With the rise of grouse shooting over the last couple of centuries, the red grouse (slightly smaller than its black relation) has come to be the main bird species of the heather moorlands of northern England and Scotland. The consequent management of moorland in such a way as to foster the red grouse has historically led to trouble in some areas between landowners and their tenants over the keeping of sheep on the hills and moors, because large numbers of sheep can kill the heather on which the grouse depend for their food, and hence their survival. When it was discovered that grouse shooting was worth a lot more money than the sheep, tenants and their sheep were sometimes tossed off the moorland, or the number of sheep they were allowed to run on it was restricted.

To start with the birds were walked up and shot over dogs. Then grouse driving of a sort began around 1804–5, when on some Yorkshire moors grouse were driven in a fashion over the guns concealed behind some rocks or small ridges. The invention of the breech-loading shotgun around 1854 made loading and firing much quicker, and between 1850 and 1870 grouse driving became well established in the north, although on some moors there were fierce battles between grouse-shooters, miners and shepherds, who didn't want the grouse shot. In Weardale they sang a song, 'They will fight till they die for the bonny moor hen'.

Around the same period the spread of the railways provided much improved travel between the north and south of England and Scotland, and many moneyed southerners were keen to travel north and spend their holidays grouse-shooting. This, of course, intensified the economic advantages of driven grouse-shooting over sheep-farming in the uplands.

And this, in turn, led to the evolution of methods of land management intended to favour the red grouse and increase its numbers. These involved improving its habitat, and one major way of doing this was by heather-burning.

Burning strips of patches of old rank heather is carried out between October or November and March or April (there are geographical differences in burning season), and a special licence is needed for burning outside these dates. Given the frequency of strong winds and rain in winter and spring, burning is not always feasible, but, particularly from late January to the end of March, keepers and their helpers tend to make use of every dry day for it. Long strips some 25 to 30 metres wide are burned, if possible spread fairly equally over the moor. The aim is to burn off old, long heather that no longer provides the birds with much food or shelter from the weather, so that it will then regrow over time.

The burning is done in strips so that anywhere on the moor there will be, within a short distance, heather of different ages and length. There will be strips of newly burnt ground, where the grouse can sun themselves and feed on the young shoots as the heather starts to regrow. There will be short heather giving cover for chicks as they forage for insects. There will be longer heather for nesting and feeding on the seed; and there will be deepish, sturdy heather, for protection from driving rain, sleet, hail and snow.

How often a strip of heather should be burnt depends a great deal on the lie of the land. Some are burnt every five to eight years or more. But there may be a tendency for some gamekeepers to under-burn rather than over-burn, for it can be very difficult to work gun dogs through very old rank heather when walking up, and it can also be very difficult for them to find shot birds in it after a drive.

Drainage on the hills and moors is another aspect of their management. It is necessary to provide enough water for birds and animals to drink, but yet you need to prevent the formation of boggy areas that make a poor habitat for them. Streams, burns and ditches may have to be cleaned out in places, and this can be a lot of work. Sheep and deer on the hills keep to certain tracks more or less all the time, and the routes they follow to their eating, drinking and lying up areas are likely to cross streams, ditches and springs. Particularly in bad weather, this can result in water courses becoming blocked or diverted. I know some moor gamekeepers who carry a spade with them more often than they carry a gun at certain times of year as they try to keep the fresh-water streams running freely. Sometimes, though, the keeper has to dam up a stream and divert the water somewhere else, so that fresh water is available to the wildlife all across the moor.

———•·———

The curlew is a bird that keeps following me around, or else I seem to keep following it around, as I meet up with this wading bird at various times of the year. For most of the year it is a coastal bird, but in the breeding season from April to July it becomes a hill and moorland bird, and its time clock tells it when to move on, no matter what the weather conditions. The curlew is the largest British wading bird and is about 18 inches (45 cm) long, from the top of its long curved beak to its tail. Its long legs and grey brown plumage make it quite easy to recognize. The bird's usual cry, *coor-lee*, which gives rise to its name, is one of the characteristic spring sounds on the moors, as is its sharp alarm call that gives it its Scottish name of whaup.

The female curlew may lay three or four pear-shaped eggs, a sort of olive green with brown marks, in a big saucer-shaped nest in long dry grass on quite open ground on the moor. Both parents share the incubation of the eggs, and when the chicks hatch out (after about four weeks), will boldly defend them against any predators. The young curlews can fly after about five weeks or so.

I go pheasant shooting to an estate up on the Scottish Border near Gretna Green, a stone's throw from the Solway Firth, and every December and January the curlews come and stand around in the nearby pastures in flocks just a field or two away from where we are shooting. They feed on the Solway estuary and shoreline first thing in the morning, probing the soft mud with their long beaks for worms, shrimps and small shellfish. When they have eaten they fly inland to a farmer's field just a short distance from the shoreline, and then they stand around in their hundreds for the rest of the day, mixing and chattering, before returning to the estuaries in the evening.

As it is soon dark in the late afternoons in December and January, the curlews collect together and begin pairing up, ready for their spring migration to the uplands to breed, and it is these that I meet up with again a month or two later when they are rearing a new family.

———•———

Another wading bird I have long known both on the farm and on the moors is the lapwing, known among farmers and country folk as the peewit, from the sound of its call. It is a smaller wading bird than the curlew and has a black-and-white appearance with a short bill and rounded wings. The peewit, too, has a regular routine, wintering on the coast and breeding inland; they can be found on farmland, moors, parks, reservoirs, bogs, marshes and estuaries.

The habitat of the peewit has changed over the years. Not so many years ago farmers used to plough the fields in the winter, from about October onwards, and the ploughed land was then left for the hard frosts to break down the soil, and the following spring the land would be harrowed and the corn sown and later the ground would be rolled to push any surface stones down into the soil (where they wouldn't damage the cutting bar of the binder when harvest time came round in the autumn). When the new-sown corn came up through the ground the pairs of peewits would arrive from the coasts and estuaries to nest in the corn fields. The male would make several small scrapes in the ground, and the female would choose a scrape and lay four dark brown eggs with dark markings on them.

By the time the ploughman was sent to roll the corn fields he was told to watch out for the peewits' nests, and sometimes he would arrive back at the farm with a dozen peewit eggs (he would take one or two from different nests and never rob any one nest entirely). He would give my mother six or eight and we would have them fried with a bit of home-cured bacon; they were slightly smaller than a bantams egg and very good eating.

The peewit is a friend to the farmers as it feeds on insects on the farmland and on the fringes of the moors, where it also nests. The incubation period of the eggs is between three and four weeks, and the young leave the nest as soon as they are dry. They can be very difficult to see, because of the excellent camouflage provided by their black-and-tan mottled down.

From the summer between July and August the birds and their growing young start grouping up into flocks. Peewits are night feeders, and flocks of them will often land in a field on the fringe of the moor and rest there all day; others may frequent reservoir edges. As winter approaches they gradually leave the higher ground and head back to the coast or to lakes, reservoirs and river valleys. Some of them migrate to Ireland from Britain, and some peewits from the Continent come and winter in Britain.

Farming changes have affected peewit numbers. Very little spring-sown corn is grown on the farms today; it is mainly autumn-sown barley, wheat, oilseed rape and various other crops, like linseed and lavender. With these, no sooner has the crop been harvested and the straw baled and removed than the fields are cultivated over and resown for next year. Some smaller farms still grow a field or two of corn, ploughing the land in the winter and sowing the corn in the spring, and there are still a few spring corn fields where peewits can still nest and rear a family, but there are fewer peewits on the farms now than there used to be.

10

The Changing Countryside

I have lived in the countryside all my life and have seen many changes, some for the better, some for the worse. One factor has been that it seems more and more of the general public want to visit the countryside for a wide range of reasons – to take part in country sports, to walk, to visit country houses, to visit wildlife sites or county shows, or just to have a picnic. Another influence has been changes in farming and the effects of EU membership. When we import so much food from abroad, it seems so strange that land is being 'set aside' to grow nothing, and farmers are paid for not growing food on it.

Looking back to around the late 1950s and 1960s, farmers never had the chemicals and fertilizers that we have today to spray crops with and to put on the land. All the animal manure from the previous winter on the farm was spread onto the land and ploughed in, and that was all the feed the crops got year after year.

The corn we used to grow on the farm was sown early in spring. Before sowing, though, the seed corn was tipped onto the granary floor, and we used to sprinkle it with a pink powder known as derris powder and mix that through the seeds with a shovel; this was to stop the birds, mice, rats and insects from eating the seeds before they started to come up. Then, when the corn was cut and threshed in the autumn and winter, some of the new seed was kept back to be dressed with the pink powder and sown the following spring. Every few years new seed corn was brought in to change the variety.

Other crops grown on the farm for cattle food were beans, potatoes, turnips and sometimes a few rows of cabbages. The root crops were eaten in the house as well as being used for cattle food. The land was ploughed every year and the different crops sown or planted on a rotational basis: one field might be sown with corn this year and then planted with potatoes the next, and so on.

All the manure from the farm's cattle, horses, pigs and poultry was also spread on the fields on a rotation, so that the land didn't get sick and tired. So, too, was lime. Spreading lime on the land was quite fashionable in the 1950s and 1960s, and it is still spread on some farms today; it sweetened the soil.

This was as good organic farming as I know, although we didn't get the heavy crops that the farmers can produce today using top-quality seeds and fertilizers. The food UK farmers produce today is top-quality, and they deserve to get paid more for it.

The 1960s and 1970s were quite good for farming. Some farmers were expanding; crops such as oats, wheat and barley were improving with the introduction of new seed varieties, and cattle breeding in the countryside was progressing with the introduction of the artificial insemination (AI) of cattle.

Many small farmers in the North Pennines in those days had bred their own stock bull from the cattle they had, producing poor, scruffy-looking cattle. But when they started using the AI service, introducing the bloodlines of top-quality pedigree bulls from other parts of the country, their cattle improved enormously in a short time. Milk yields rose markedly and so did the quality of the breeding stock and the beef cattle.

The small farmers in the North Pennines were great people to go and visit and when I was working for the Milk Marketing Board they always made me very welcome – the kettle was always on the boil. It was great to be involved with them. I saw many young families grow up in the Dales and am still very friendly with lots of them.

Life wasn't a bed of roses for these small dairy, beef and sheep farmers. Times could be very hard for most families, and some northern winters, with the heavy falls of snow, and bitter hard frosts and perishing winds were real killers, because sometimes the winter weather went on well into the spring.

Some farms could be cut off for weeks at a time by heavy snowfalls that blocked off the farm access roads.

I well remember the real hard winter of 1974. Arctic weather with heavy snow and penetrating frosts that went on and on and never seemed to let up. At the time I was travelling around the small farms in Tynedale in a Land Rover. I was in Alston in Cumberland one really hard winter's day, and it was snowing like hell. I was going to see a small farmer in Garrigill, a small village about five miles away, and as I struggled over the shoulder of Middle Fell on the way there it was snowing so heavily I could hardly see where I was going. Halfway over I met the snow plough, straining against the cold to keep the road open, and paused for a word with the crew, who advised me to get the hell out of there while I could. I tried to push on but I could hardly see; I got stuck in a deep snowdrift about two miles from Garrigill. As I struggled to extricate myself, I burnt out the Land Rover's clutch, I was freezing cold and the light was beginning to fade.

I wrapped up as best I could against the arctic cold and the blizzard wind, the snow blowing so hard that I could hardly see a metre or so ahead, and set off on foot. By the time I had struggled down to the village my gloves were frozen onto my hands. I kicked on the hotel door and the surprised lady owner who opened it quickly helped me get the frozen gloves off and start warming up again. I was soon in a bath, then had something to eat and finally, after a drop or two of whisky, felt quite well.

Next morning the weather was no better, and all the roads were still blocked with deep snow, but I decided to struggle the five miles back to Alston on foot, and there got the train back to Hexham in Northumberland; it was quite an ordeal. My Land Rover was stuck between Alston and Garrigill for over four weeks before the mechanics were able to tow it into the garage and repair it.

Those very hard winters we used to get in the north in the 1960s, 1970s and 1980s also badly affected our shooting. The heavy snowfalls made it nearly impossible to get around on some shoots, and it wasn't safe to be out with guns and dogs in such conditions.

We frequently got heavy snow covering the moors in early November or before, which disrupted the grouse shooting and often put a stop to it a month or so before the end of the season. Pheasant shooting, too, was often hit by the snow and blizzards; it wasn't safe to be game shooting or working the dogs when conditions were so bad and the snow was blowing into my face and into the dogs' faces, and the snow was too deep to walk through.

We don't get such very hard winters in the north any more, although we probably have more wind and rain. We still get very wet, windy days when we have to pack up shooting earlier in the day than we normally would. However, on the whole those very hard winters in many ways were much better for us all – apart from having frozen water pipes in the cowsheds, and the cows bellowing their heads off for a drink, so that the pipes had to be thawed out several times a night. The hard weather killed off many bugs and diseases. (The downside, though, was that lots of small birds in the countryside died of starvation.)

As farming started expanding in the 1970s there was a great demand for British food, and we also joined the Common Market. As a result, the countryside started to change a lot to produce this extra food, although I don't really know if the changes were all good, for many small farmers went out of business at that time.

Many hedgerows and stone walls were pulled out or pulled down to make bigger fields in which to grow more food. There were a few court cases to try and stop some farmers and landowners cutting down plantations and pulling out trees to enlarge their fields so as to grow barley and wheat more efficiently and use the new agricultural machinery that was also getting bigger and more efficient. But removing the hedge and walls removed the nesting sites for many small birds and animals.

Some of the wildlife took a great knock in the 1980s from changes to its habitat, as many small corners of the countryside were ploughed out and planted with barley and wheat. One bird in particular that we have lost in many parts of the north is the corncrake, a slim, brown bird with a short deep bill and bright chestnut wings. We have removed its ground cover and habitat, and it has just disappeared altogether from many parts of the countryside.

This shy bird wasn't often seen in the open, but nearly sixty years ago I used to hear the lovely rasping call of the male corncrake every spring in the hay fields. The female laid eight to twelve brownish-red spotted eggs in a well-hidden nest; she incubated them for just over two weeks, and it was about another four weeks before the young birds could fly. I very often used to try to flush the corncrakes with my gun dogs or try to find their nests in the old pastures where there was plenty of long grass and cover. Corncrakes would often nest in dry bogs where there were plenty of rushes and long grass.

Changes in agriculture and agricultural machinery are most to blame for the birds' decline. The old reaper or hay-cutting bar left a stubble of grass about six to eight inches (15–20 cm) high, and any birds sitting on eggs were quite safe (as long as they ducked their heads when the grass cutting bar was coming). But the new hay cutting machines chopped the grass right down to the soil, and any sitting birds such as corncrakes, pheasants or partridges were just chopped to bits. The corncrakes couldn't stand their habitat being destroyed every spring and left for pastures new, where there are still rough meadows and bogs that are not disturbed year after year.

There are some corncrakes coming back to parts of northern England and the north and west of Scotland and to some of the Western Isles, and the birds are still quite common in parts of Ireland where they have small fields and cut their hay with the old-fashioned reaper that leaves plenty of grass stubble.

The birds' welcome return may have something to do with the way changes in agriculture have affected the cattle to which the hay used to be fed in the winter. Dairy farmers in the UK are not doing very well nowadays, as they are not getting paid enough money for the milk they produce. Every week there are farmers having to sell their dairy herds because of the poor returns they are getting, and in the last couple of years some 6,000 of them have got out of dairying.

I can well remember there were about 50,000 dairy farmers in England and Wales in the 1970s, when the Milk Marketing Board was operating and guaranteed them a stable price for the milk they produced. Then we joined the Common Market, and the Board was seen as a monopoly, and so had to be abolished. Dairy farmers lost the security it provided and had to sort out their own marketing, and today there are under 14,000 dairy farmers in England and Wales.

Meanwhile, beef producers have not had it easy either, particularly in recent years. In 1986 they were hit by an epidemic of Bovine Spongiform Encephalopathy (BSE, or 'Mad Cow Disease'), which is normally fatal to cattle and is capable of being transmitted to humans who have eaten meat from affected animals in the form of new variant Creutzfeldt-Jakob Disease. More than 183,000 cases of BSE in cattle have been confirmed in the UK since the epidemic was first identified, with some 200 human deaths from CJD. The BSE epidemic peaked in the early 1990s at around 37,000 cases a year, or roughly three cows in every hundred.

In 1996 all exports of British beef were banned, and great strides were taken by the farming industry to reduce the number of animals affected by the disease, but it would be another ten years or so before various beef restrictions were lifted. Today beef cattle being produced by the UK farmers are of top quality, and the beef is once again really worth buying.

Then in 2001 Foot and Mouth disease (which affects not only cattle but also sheep, goats and pigs) cropped up again in the UK and cost the country millions and the enforced slaughter of

ten million animals, which might have been miti-
gated if animal movement restrictions had taken
effect sooner.

So, the agricultural industry has been
changing at a great pace, as other industries –
such as coal, steel and shipbuilding – have done
before it. And they have almost gone, whether
that is good for the country or not.

The government is now paying landowners
and farmers for not growing so much food as they
did, because a great variety of food can now be
imported from Europe and all over the world. So
they must diversify away from food production.

What you can diversify into and what to do
with your farm buildings really depend on where
your farm is based.

If it is near a country village or a town, where
there is lots of passing traffic, then a farm shop
selling local produce, with a coffee shop alongside, is an ideal business to diversify into. And
farmers growing acres of soft fruits, such as
strawberries, raspberries, blackcurrants and
gooseberries, can ask the general public to come
and pick their own fruits. Again, though, the
farm has to be situated near where people are
passing; it is not much good having a pick-your-
own fruit farm miles from anywhere that
anybody ever goes to.

Converting some of your farm buildings into riding stables, with ponies for young children learning to ride, is another good money-spinning diversification. In this case your farm can be further away from passing traffic, as people often expect riding stables to be out in the countryside. (It doesn't have to be, though. I know a few farmers running stables where the farm is just outside a town or village, and the stables are run as part of the farming business.) And having a working farm that is open to the general public is another way for farmers to earn money, and also to educate the general public about where their food comes from and about the wildlife of the countryside.

The fields and fields of yellow-flowered crops you see in the countryside are likely to be oilseed rape, which produces an edible oil that is used for making margarine, for baking with, as a cooking and salad oil and for making biodiesel fuel. Some of the farmers who grow oilseed rape are now diversifying crushing the rapeseed themselves, bottling the oil and selling it to shops and super-markets. And some farmers in southern England are trying to grow crops normally imported from abroad, such as olives and apricots, in the belief that the process of climate change will favour this form of diversification.

For years some members of the general public have thought that UK farmers were being subsidized by the taxpayer to run around in Range Rovers and Jaguars.

Far from it! If some farmers producing food to feed the nation hadn't had a subsidy from the government then many of them would have gone bust – because they weren't getting enough money from the market for the food they produced. Now, though, as members of the Common Market, we can no longer pay UK farmers subsidies for producing the food they do. Farmers and growers can now export or import their unsubsidized produce to or from any country in the Common Market, provided they can sell it and each country deals with their own farmers regards payments.

From 2005 the system of subsidies to UK farmers was replaced by a Single Farm Payment scheme, and this runs until the year 2012. Under this, government payments are related to the land itself, and not to whatever crops are grown on it. This opens the way to treating environmental protection or improvement as an object in itself (almost as if it had been a crop), and there are now quite a few government schemes that the farmers can join. They can involve looking after the environment on the farm; looking after the wildlife habitat; looking after the stone walls; looking after the ditches, trees and hedges; and so on. They are based on a points system – you get so many points for looking after hay meadows, for filling gaps in hedgerows, repairing stone walls, etc. and you can get some free advice from the Heritage Trust to start with.

On my farm I have joined the Environment Stewardship Scheme and look after my oak trees, hay meadows, and hedges. All the government schemes pay a little bit of money, and as the year 2012 approaches, apart from helping to look after the environment, the extra money coming onto the farm will be a great help. So the future of the changing countryside looks good.